I0834808

A HISTORY *of* ELIZABETHTOWN, KENTUCKY

AND ITS SURROUNDINGS

BY

SAMUEL HAYCRAFT

(Written in 1869)

PUBLISHED BY

THE WOMAN'S CLUB *of* ELIZABETHTOWN, KY.

1921

Notice

In many older books, foxing (or discoloration) occurs and, in some instances, print lightens with wear and age. Reprinted books, such as this, often duplicate these flaws, notwithstanding efforts to reduce or eliminate them. The pages of this reprint have been digitally enhanced and, where possible, the flaws eliminated in order to provide clarity of content and a pleasant reading experience.

A History of Elizabethtown, Kentucky,
And Its Surroundings

Originally published
Elizabethtown, Kentucky
1921

Reprinted by:

Janaway Publishing, Inc.
732 Kelsey Ct.
Santa Maria, California 93454
(805) 925-1038
www.janawaygenealogy.com

2010

ISBN 10: 1596412003
ISBN 13: 9781596412002

Made in the United States of America

The history ends abruptly with a short sketch of Ben Hardin which it was evidently intended to continue. It is to be hoped that the example of this history will stimulate some later public spirited citizen to continue the history of the town down to the present day.

For the privilege of publishing this history the Woman's Club is indebted to Mr. H. A. Sommers and the other owners of the Elizabethtown News and takes pleasure in expressing here its obligations to them.

THE WOMAN'S CLUB OF ELIZABETHTOWN, KY.

MISS LILLIE GOLDNAMER,
MISS EMILY PAYNE,
MISS MARGARET STEWART,
MRS. W. H. ROBERTSON,
MRS. J. R. SELBY,
MRS. R. W. CATES,
MRS. R. B. PARK,
Committee.

PRELIMINARY NOTE

Samuel Haycraft's "History of Elizabethtown and Its Surroundings" was published in the Elizabethtown News in 1869 and republished in 1889-90. The preservation of this history through its publication in the News is a happy occurrence, for in no other way would much of the early history of the town have been accurately preserved.

Mr. Haycraft was a son of one of the three pioneer settlers of the town, and was born when the town was still an early pioneer settlement. At the time of his death he had lived here 83 years, and he was the only remaining citizen whose life went back to the town's earliest days. Elizabethtown is now 140 years old, and it will not be long before no one will be left whose interest in the town's history is quickened by personal memory of its early inhabitants. When that time comes, traditions will rapidly grow vague, and the knowledge of its early history and characters will be lost. On account of facts like these the Elizabethtown Woman's Club undertook the publication of Haycraft's History in book form. The original suggestion of this came from Mrs. William Allen Pusey, of Chicago. There are many Elizabethtown people both at home and abroad to whom the town is dear and who are interested in preserving its history. When this matter was proposed to them there was a gratifying response which has enabled the club to proceed with the undertaking.

Quite aside from local interest and personal feelings there are other good reasons for the publication of this work. It is an exceedingly interesting document, particularly in the vivid description which the writer gives of pioneer customs and conditions. The author loved the town and its early history, and he describes it in vigorous style and with a quaint sense of humor. He was little disturbed in his writing by the laws of composition, but his descriptions flow on easily, and the reader is never uncertain as to what he is trying to say. The original copy has been reproduced without any effort at alteration or correction. A few chapters, composed of material not really a part of the history of the town and its surroundings, have been omitted.

Samuel Haycraft

Taken in Sept. 1877, in his 83d year

Sarah B. Haycraft

Taken in 1872, in her 73d year

SAMUEL HAYCRAFT

Samuel Haycraft was born August 14, 1795, in Elizabethtown, Kentucky, in a double, round-log cabin. His father was Samuel Haycraft, a Revolutionary soldier, and a man of great public and private worth, who settled in Kentucky early in the latter quarter of the eighteenth century. His mother was Margaret VanMeter, daughter of Jacob VanMeter, and belonged to one of the old and honorable pioneer families of the State. The subject of this sketch, one of the most remarkable men who ever lived in Elizabethtown, spent nearly seven years of his boyhood in the country schools, the last two chiefly in studying the Latin language. He was a careful, discriminating, and extensive reader, and few men of the country were so thoroughly and universally well informed. His long public career commenced when he was fourteen years of age. At that time, in October, 1809, he began to write in the office of the County and Circuit Clerk, Major Ben Helm. The duties of this position he performed, with little variation, until 1816, when he received the appointment of Clerk of both Circuit and County Courts of Hardin County, and held this clerkship, uninterruptedly, until 1857. He said of himself, "That, from the time he entered this office, he was attentive to business, and never neglected it; but, in leisure moments, was fond of gay and lively company, particularly of dancing parties, but hardly ever descended to low company or rowdyism, but was a wild, wicked sinner." On retiring from this office, in 1851, the court and bar adopted, and placed on record, resolutions in every way flattering to him in his official capacity, as well as social and private relations of life.

He, then, began the practice of law at the Elizabethtown bar; but after four years of legal practice, was again called by the people to fill the vacant clerkship of the Circuit Court, caused by the death of the incumbent. In 1857 he was elected to represent the people in the State Senate and held this position for four years. He was, therefore, a member of the Legislature during the most important and critical period of the State's history. His record made in that body was most honorable to himself, and, in the light of the present, is stamped by a wisdom, foresight, and fearless devotion to just and true principles, of which any man might well be proud. He was instrumental in enacting some measures beneficial to the general good; and it was through his efforts, mainly, that the Legislature was induced to appropriate even the meagre sum it did for the erection of a monument to Daniel Boone. And, in that body, he was one of the most determined and staunch supporters of the Union. He was then sixty-seven years of age, and had lived with his father through the greater part of the life-time of the nation, and now stood in the Senate, gray with time and honor, one of the noblest Romans of them all, ever ready to say, "The Union must and shall be preserved." But neither in that august body nor among his friends and neighbors at home, was he ever obnoxious in his opinions; on the contrary, however, conciliatory, generous and discriminating, claiming only to himself his private opinions, and deeply sympathizing with the troubles of his neighbors and the evils and misfortunes of the times. He was again elected Clerk of the Circuit Court and retired in 1868, at the age of seventy-three, after an unparalleled service of sixty-five years. He said of himself that "On the first Saturday in April, 1832, my wife and I were baptized by Elder Warren Cash, who also married us; and, in answer to my mother's prayers, she lived to see all her children in the Church, and to hear her youngest son preach the Gospel." For over forty years he was a member of the Baptist Church, a teacher in the Sabbath-schools and observed family prayers twice a day. For several years he was a Trustee of Georgetown College, to which he made some bequests. Of himself, he says: "I have occupied the same seat in church for over forty years, and never sit back in the scorner's place. On the 29th of October, 1818, I was married to Sarah Brown Helm, a daughter of Judge John Helm, of Breckinridge County. I regard the transaction as the most fortunate move of my life, temporally speaking." They had four children: Edgar H., DeSoto, Iowa; Sarah M., wife of S. McMurtry, Hardin County; Louisa Ann, wife of William Dix, Breckinridge County; and Margaret J., wife of C. D. Poston, once Representative in Congress from Arizona. Mr. Haycraft was a fine public speaker and one of the most interesting conversationalists. His disposition to joke was inveterate and a vein of humor seemed to underlie the most serious moments of his life. He was a man of fine address, most genial temperament, courteous manner and splendid personal appearance; and few men of his age showed such high preservation of all the noble elements of manhood. He stood as a monument of the effects of correct principles and practices of life, both physically and mentally. Yet he modestly said: "My life has been rather quiet and monotonous, and does not afford much matter for history, especially of an extraordinary character."

He evidently found pleasure in composition on subjects which were of interest to him; these were especially the pioneer times and people, his church, and religion. He not infrequently wrote letters to the Louisville papers, and was an occasional contributor to religious publications. In Ford's Christian Repository of May, 1875, pp. 350 to 361 he has an autobiography. In the same of October, 1875, pp. 276 to 285 there is a sermon by him.

This history was probably suggested to him by an investigation which he made and embodied in a very interesting "Letter to the churches comprising the Salem Association of United Baptists" read at Big Spring meeting house September 22nd, 1871. Although read after the publication of his history, the context shows that it was prepared in 1843.

His wife died August 14th, 1878. They had been married 60 years, lacking two months. To her he repeatedly paid tribute throughout his career, and she was as much of a character in the town as he was. A gentle, generous, pious woman of the old generation she was "Aunt Sallie" to the whole community. Many of us still remember her agreeable peculiarity of always having on hand "sweet cakes" for distribution to the children who came to her house. She and her husband lived in the fine square colonial brick house that stood on the northeast corner of Main and Poplar Streets, the first brick house erected in Elizabethtown. Two magnificent magnolia trees stood on either side of the portico. It was a house of character, and it was a loss to the town when it was destroyed by fire about 1882.

He followed his wife to the grave in his 84th year on December 22nd, 1878, four months after her death.

COPY OF A LETTER WRITTEN PRIOR TO LINCOLN'S ELECTION TO PRESIDENCY

Following is a letter which came into the possession of Mrs. W. H. Courtney, Owensboro, Ky., written by Lincoln to Hon. Samuel Haycraft, grandfather of Mrs. Courtney, just prior to his election in 1860:

Springfield, Ill., Aug. 16, 1860.

Hon. Samuel Haycraft,
Elizabethtown, Ky.

My Dear Sir:

A correspondent of the New York Herald, who was here a week writing to that paper, represents me as saying I have been invited to visit Kentucky, but that I suspected it was a trap to inveigle me into Kentucky in order to do violence to me.

This is wholly a mistake. I said no such thing. I do not remember, but I possibly did mention my correspondence with you, but very certainly I was not guilty of stating or intimating a suspicion of any intended violence, deception, or other wrong against me by you or any other Kentuckian.

Thinking this Herald correspondence must reach you, I think it due to myself to enter my protest against this part of it.

I scarcely think the correspondent was malicious, but rather that he misused what was said.

Yours very truly,

A. LINCOLN.

CHAPTER I

Having been requested by you to furnish my recollections of Elizabethtown, I cheerfully comply with your request. Although born in it seventy-four years ago, in order to furnish a history of the town and its founders, I shall be compelled to draw a little upon tradition, running back to the fall of 1779, in order to give a just idea of the kind of men, their mode of life, etc., who first came to the valley in which the town is situated. My father and mother being among the very first, enables me to speak with some certainty, as I received it from them.

Elizabethtown is situated in Hardin county, on the southern slope of Muldraughs Hill, and Severn's Valley creek, a branch of Nolin, which empties into Green river. The town is ten miles southwest of the Beech and Rolling Fork of Salt river, forty-two miles from Louisville, by the Louisville and Nashville railroad, and forty-five miles by the way of the Louisville and Nashville turnpike road, and those two roads cross at right angles in Elizabethtown.

The valley took its name from John Severns, an early adventurer, who, being attracted by the beauty of the location, entered land, and gave the name to the creek and valley. The head waters of Valley creek, and Rawlings' fork, each about three or four miles long, form a junction in the town, where it takes the name of Severn's Valley creek. This beautiful stream, in its course downward, is fed by Shaw's creek, Billy's creek, East and West Rhude's creeks, and by numerous never-failing springs of limpid water, cool and refreshing. About eight miles below town it disembogues into the stream of Nolin. The whole stream is about twelve miles long. The valley through which it runs varies from two to seven miles wide. The greater part, particularly that portion surrounding the town, was originally a dense forest of heavy timber. Poplar, walnut, sugar maple, wild cherry, hackberry, plum, etc., and various other growths, and undergrowths of spice wood, leather wood, etc., indicating the richest soil. The greater portion of this beautiful and fertile valley was taken by John Severns, Andrew Hynes,

Thomas Helm, Joseph Stover, Jacob Funk, Claudius Paul Raguet, Osburn Spriggs, John Handley, Jacob Harris, and others not now remembered. It was then in Jefferson county, and belonged to the old mother of States, Virginia—afterwards it was divided and became Nelson county.

On the 1st day of June, 1792, Kentucky was made a State by the consent of Virginia; and in 1793 Hardin county was founded, bounded by the Ohio river, Salt river, Rolling fork to Salt Lick, striking across the hills to Green river, and down the river to the Ohio, embracing all the counties of Hardin, Meade, Breckinridge, Davies and Ohio, and the great parts of Hart, Grayson and part of Edmonson.

About the fall of 1779 and winter of 1780, the early settlers were Captain Thomas Helm, Colonel Andrew Hynes and Samuel Haycraft; each of these persons built forts with block houses. The forts were stockades, constructed of split timber—then deemed sufficient for defense against the Indian rifles. The sites were well selected, each on elevated ground, commanding springs of never failing and excellent water.

The forts formed a triangle, equidistant a mile apart. Captain Helm's fort occupied the hill on which Governor Helm's residence now stands. Colonel Hynes' was on the elevation now occupied by J. H. Bryan, formerly by Ambrose Geoghegan, Sen., and for many years by John H. Geoghegan, Esq. Haycraft's fort was on the hill above the Cave spring, in which the flesh of many a deer, buffalo and bear were preserved for use, as salt in these days were not to be had. There were no other settlements at that time between the falls of the Ohio and Green river. Those forts were subject to frequent attacks by the Indians. The report of a gun at either of these forts was the signal by which the other forts were warned of the danger and summoned to the aid of the beseiged fortress, which was promptly responded to. Many were the inroads made by savages upon the infant settlements at that early period. Soon after a hardy set of adventurers came in and settled around the forts, consisting of the Millers, Vertreeses, Vanmeters, Harts, Shaws, Dyers, &c., who assisted in repelling the attacks of the Indians. Many deeds of daring valor were performed by those sturdy pioneers. It cost some blood. Henry Helm, son of old Captain Thomas Helm, was killed; also Dan Vertrees, the honored grandfather of Judge W. D. Vertees, our fellow-citizen. Dan Vertrees was a stalwart young man of daring. He, with the late Colonel Nicholas Miller and others, were pursuing a band of Indians; Miller, then young, was tall, slenderly built, as active as a cat, and as fleet as hind, and as brave as Julius Caesar. This company coming upon the Indians, suddenly, a desperate fight ensued. Vertrees was killed at the first fire. A stout warrior seized a white man, wrestled his gun from him and was about to cleve his head with an axe. Miller at that moment, with a celerity of action which few men could equal, and with a power that few possessed —in the language of John Glenn, "snatched the white man from the Indian as he would a chicken from a hawk," and, with an equal rapid motion, killed the Indian: This turned the tide, and the remaining Indians fled, leaving several dead on the ground.

Miles Hart, while defending his domicile with an open door, springing from side to side, loading and firing, and keeping at bay a band of savages for a considerable length of time, was finally killed, and his wife and two children taken prisoners. It may not be uninteresting to note a circumstance showing the capability of endurance possessed by those early settlers. Mrs. Elizabeth Hart, the widow of Miles Hart, was regarded as a very delicate woman for those days. She was enceinte when taken a prisoner—in an advanced state. She was burdened with camp kettles and other Indian plunder; they crossed the Ohio river into the Northwestern territory. After journeying a few days, at nightfall, she was compelled to kindle the Indian fires, and then made to go aside and kindle a fire for herself, raking up as best she could rubbish from under the snow, and there alone, unaided by the kind assistance known to civilized life, was delivered of a son. The squaws then showed a little kindness in the morning, by giving her a little water in which a turkey had been boiled. Then cutting a block from a tree, they wrapped a piece of blanket around the new-born infant, fastened it to the block, and laid the block upon her back with camp kettles, &c., and pursued their way, and, in the course of a day, waded a river waist deep, and yet, strange to tell, she experienced no serious inconvenience but from hard usages and inhuman treatment, the child died at six months old.

She lingered in captivity and wretched slavery for several years, until a trading Frenchman at Detroit purchased her from the Indians, and restored her to her relations. She afterwards married and raised a considerable family. Bailey T. Price, Mrs. Thomas Tabb, and Mrs. John Tabb, are her grand children, and now live among us.

Another instance to show the hardships of the people of those days: On the 25th day of December, 1780, the late Benjamin Helm, Esq., then a lad of fourteen years of age (son of Captain Thomas Helm), walked barefooted to the falls of the Ohio (now Louisville) for meal or salt. Mr. Helm afterwards lived to an advanced age, over ninety years! He died some years ago, a wealthy and highly esteemed old gentleman, of the old school, having spent a life of sobriety, honesty and industry, having filled the offices of Circuit and County Court Clerks many years, and various other respectable stations, and was justly considered a benefactor in the community; built the Methodist Church here almost unaided, and died a member of it—a true Christian.

On the 17th day of June, 1781, under the shadow of a green sugar tree, near Haynes' station, a Baptist church was constituted with eighteen members, by Elder William Taylor and Joseph Barnett, preachers, with Elder John Gerrard, who was ordained first pastor. The church was called the Regular Baptist Church of Severn's Valley. The same church still exists in Elizabethtown and is known by the name of the United Baptist Church of Jesus Christ, called Severn's Valley, and is now the oldest Baptist church that maintains an existence in Kentucky. All the members and preacher emigrated from Virginia, and Elder Gerrard might have been emphatically styled, "the voice of one crying in the wilderness."

This man of God was only permitted to exercise the functions of his office for nine months. For in common with his friends he was compelled to seek the game of the forest for a living, and being with a hunting party they were surprised by a band of Indians, all except Elder Gerrard made their escape, he being lame, was taken, and whether he was slain outright, burnt at the stake, or lingered in captivity was never known, and like Moses the place of his sepulchre is not known to this day. He left a family and his decendants, the Millers and Thomases, are among us to this day. The elder and younger Jacob Vanmeter and the wife of the elder were in the original constitution of the church. The decendants of the first Jacob Vanmeter now number upwards of 3,000 and are scattered over nearly all the States of the Union. He was my grandfather; he died on the 16th day of November, 1798, and was buried on his own farm, now owned by George Strickler. A plain stone of sand rock now marks the spot, the letters on it all legible, though of seventy years' standing.

CHAPTER II

Church going folks of the present day who make it a point to appear in their best attire at the public religious services might feel some curiosity to know how our ancestors appeared on such occasions and I hope they will not blush at the description.

I received my information from Jacob Vanmeter, who was the younger Jacob Vanmeter in the original constitution of the church. He died a few years since at the advanced age of about ninety-five, having been a Baptist eighty-four years.

They then had no house of worship. In the summertime they worshipped in the open air, in the winter time they met in the round log cabins with dirt floors, as there was no mills and plank to make a floor. A few who had aspired to be a little aristocratic split timber and made puncheon floors.

The men dressed as Indians; leather leggins and moccasins adorned their feet and legs. Hats made of splinters rolled in Buffalo wool and sewed together with deer sinews or buckskin whang; shirts of buckskin and hunting shirts of the same; some went the whole Indian costume and wore breech-clouts. The females wore a coarse cloth made of Buffalo wool, underwear of dressed doe skin, sun bonnets, something after the fashion of men's hats and the never-failing moccasin for the feet in winter, in summer time all went barefooted.

When they met for preaching or prayer, the men sat with their trusty rifles at their sides, and as they had to watch as well as pray, a faithful sentinel keeping a look out for the lurking Indian. But it so happened that their services were never seriously interrupted, except on one occasion. One of the watchers came to the door hole during a sermon and endeavored by signs and winks to apprise the people that something was wrong—not being exactly understood, a person within winked at the messenger, as much as to say, "Don't interrupt us." But the case being urgent, the outside man exclaimed "None of your winking and blinking—I tell you the Indians are about."

That was understood, the meeting was closed, and military defense organized. Now, gentle and fair reader, I beseech you, not to blush or be ashamed of your forerunners; they were the chosen of God and nature's nobility. There was no distinction or turning up of noses in that day, each was his other's equal, they were brothers and so esteemed and loved each other.

No burdened field of corn; no waving fields of wheat came to the harvest; no potato crop burrowed the earth. The wild game that roamed the forest was the only dependence the first year; the rifle was indispensable. It was made common cause, food was obtained at the risk of life. The unsuccessful hunter lacked nothing. The man who brought down the buffalo, the deer or bear, divided out and all had plenty. When news reached a fort that Indians were around, all were upon the alert, the men seeing that their weapons were in order, and the women, God bless them, went each to their neighbor, and inquired, "Have you plenty of meat? If you have not I have it." And immediately there was an equal division. The dried venison, called "jirk," was the bread; the fat, juicy bear the esculent, the bulky buffalo, the substantial; and the turkey the dessert; nobody had the dyspepsia and all had good teeth. But soon the brawny arm leveled the forest fields were opened and a plenty of the substantials of life soon blessed their labors.

Often has the writer heard old people talk with great fondness of old forting times as a green spot in their history—they loved to dwell upon the scenes of early trails and dangers, when men and women were all true hearted and no selfishness.

At an early period Christopher Bush settled in the valley, in what is now the boundary of Elizabethtown. He was of German descent, a stirring, industrious man, and had a large family of sons and daughters. The sons were stalwart men, of great muscular power; there was no backout in them; never shunned a fight when they considered it necessary to engage in it, and nobody ever heard one cry "enough." The most of the family left Kentucky. One of the daughters married Thomas Lincoln, the father of the late President, Abraham Lincoln, who was the son of a former wife, and she had the principal care of rearing and educating the future President. She was an excellent woman.

Christopher Bush, Jr., the youngest son, but one of the original Christopher Bush, remained and died in Kentucky. He was a good citizen and successful farmer. He reared a family and paid more attention to the education of his children than any other member of the family, and it turns out that his labor was not in vain. His eldest son, Martin M. Bush, Esq., is one of the best surveyors in the State. The Hon. W. P. D. Bush is a lawyer of considerable distinction; he has been frequently in the Legislature of Kentucky and was in some degree a leader of the Democratic party, and is now reporter of the decisions of the Court of Appeals. Two other sons, Robert Y. Bush and Squire H. Bush, are lawyers of promise.

One of his daughters was married to Col. Martin H. Cofer. Col. Cofer, son of Thomas Cofer, was born in the vicinity of this town, and under adverse circumstances commenced the study of law, and soon after entered upon a lucrative and successful practice at the Elizabethtown bar. At the commencement of the late civil war he took sides with the Confederates and commanded a regiment throughout the war, and was regarded as an able and gallant commander and now bears upon his person some receipts that will accompany him through life. As soon as the war was ended, having passed through many of the most terrible battles of that disastrous war he returned to Elizabethtown, having lost all but his honor, and immediately applied himself assiduously to his profession, gracefully submitting himself to the laws and the powers that be, in such a manner as gave him the esteem of all parties, acknowledging that the wager of battle had decided against secession. He has since published a valuable work on the decisions of the Court of Appeals of Kentucky, and is now regarded as one of the best lawyers in Kentucky.

CHAPTER III

FIRST COURT

The first term of the county court was held at the house of Isaac Hynes on the 22nd day of July, 1793. Present, Patrick Brown, John Vertrees, Robt. Hodgen and Bladen Ashby, gentlemen Justices.

FIRST CLERK

John Paul was appointed clerk protempore, not having a certificate of qualification. Isaac Hynes produced a commission and was qualified as first sheriff. Constables, districts were laid off by captains companies. John Paul, under a commission, qualified as first coroner.

AUGUST TERM, 1793

Samuel Haycraft was appointed to take in the lists of taxable property for Hardin county.

FIRST SURVEYOR

Benjamin Helm, under a commission from Governor Shelby, qualified as surveyor.

Several constables were appointed, and as hogs and cattle began to multiply in the land, many men had their "ear-marks," meaning stock mark, recorded.

The mark recording continued for many years in great abundance, as men were honest and did not wish to take their neighbor's hogs and had a slight indisposition to losing their own.

Anticipating that some men might be poor, overseers of the poor were elected. Court house and jail talked about it. At that time an order was spread on paper, no record book being yet procured, in these words:.

"Pursuant to an act of Assembly a majority of the magistrates in the commission of the peace, were of the opinion that the most convenient place for erecting the poor house and jail for county of Hardin, was in Severn's Valley on the land belonging to Andrew Hynes, laid off for that purpose, and on that part of said land that adjoins Samuel Haycraft, and it is ordered that said building be erected at the aforesaid place. By consent of Isaac Hynes it is ordered by the court that he build a pound for the purpose of keeping strays on court days as directed by an act of Assembly."

JAIL

On the same day the sheriff was directed to let out the building of the "jail to the lowest bidder." The court adjourned to meet at the house of Isaac Hynes.

The stray pen or pound was then necessary, as few pastures were enclosed, and cattle and horses found plentiful food in browsing on the cane brakes. Cane grew in abundance on all rich lands and particularly on the margins of water courses.

I might as well say here that clerks had no office buildings, no desks or presses, or any lock up affairs. The clerk of the county court tumbled his papers into a basket. The clerk of the Quarterly session court, laid his documents in a buckeye bread tray.

No bound books; what purported to be the records were written on coarse sheets of paper sewed together. But since by authority of the Legislature acts have been transcribed into bound books.

Previous to and at this term, the court manifested a laudable zeal in opening communication with the outside world "and the rest of mankind." Viewers were appointed to lay off roads from the court house (as the town had no name) to Parepoint's mill, to the crossing of Meeting creek on the way to Hartford. And Robert Baird, Phillip Taylor and Robert Mosley were appointed to continue as viewers for a road from the crossing of Meeting creek to Hartford; these two links proposed a road seventy-five miles long, through a trackless country, except buffalo traces, and those traces had no general direction, except from cane brake and from water course to water course and celebrated licks.

DEER LICKS

Deer resorted much to salt or sulphur licks; these licks were closely watched by hunters, and as those animals are keen scented, the hunter took his position in the trees surrounding the lick, and it was a rare thing to miss bringing down a buck every night. Experienced hunters never looked for the game on the course of the wind, as a deer could smell a man on the wind two hundred yards.

ROADS

To return to roads. Ways were laid out from Hodgen's mill to the valley, to the Burnt lick on Rolling fork to Salt lick, and the road from Elizabethtown to Hodgen's mill established 75 years ago still exists with some small alterations.

JAIL

At the same time, 1793, the building of the first jail was let to Isaac La Rue at twelve pounds and sixteen shillings.

CHAPTER IV

I omitted to state in the proper place, to-wit: At July term, 1793.

"The court proceeded to rate the several ordinaries in the counties as follows:

To whisky by the half pint, 7½ pence; for lodging one night, 3 pence; for supper or breakfast, 1 shilling; for dinner, 1 shilling and 6 pence; for stabling and hay per night, 1 shilling; for corn and oats by the gallon, 6 pence; for one quart do., 2 pence; for pasturage for horses 24 hours, 6 pence.

The tavern keepers at Hartford, Vienna and Hardin's settlement (Hardinsburg) are allowed to sell whisky at 6 pence per half pint.

There is something remarkable in the above bill. One-half pint of whisky seems to have been worth two and a half nights' rest in a feather bed; perhaps whisky was considered to be a necessity, and a good night's rest a mere matter of fancy; but it is more difficult to arrive at the reason why whisky was not worth as much at Vienna (falls of Green river), Hartford or Hardin's settlement as at the Valley. It might have been because whisky was not so good at those places or money matters a little tighter, although Beaver was more plentiful at those places.

(Note—Taverns were at this date styled "ordinaries," universally pronounced "ornaries," and Spiller Waide says, "It is highly likely the pronunciation hit the nail on the head more appropriately than the spelling." In Virginia they are yet called Inns.)

BIG BILL

Speaking of Hardin's station or settlement, I digress a little. William Hardin, who founded the settlement, was a man of giant size, and ponderous weight, and was a terror to the Indians, and was known to them as "Big Bill," and their great desire was to get his scalp.

Hardin, like every other man at that day, was a hunter. Early one morning he came out of his house and fired off his gun, in order to wipe it out, preparatory to a hunt. A stout warrior stepped from behind the chimney with a rifle poised and, making sure of his man, could not resist the temptation to tantalize, and exclaimed: "Hooh, Big Bill!" That was a fatal pause for the Indian, when Hardin, quick with his gun, clubbed, knocked down the Indian's gun, and in a minute the Indian lay dead at his feet.

COUNTY LEVY

At December term, 1793, the court proceeded to lay the county levy.

The allowance amounted to 47 pounds 14 shillings, including building of the jail, clerk's book, sheriff's extra services, per cent, and in the whole county there were 318 tithables assessed at 3 shillings each.

Samuel Haycraft, gentleman, as commissioner of taxes, allowed 31 days for taking lists at 6 shillings per day.

(The county was nearly 140 miles long and on an average nearly 50 miles wide.)

Commissioner appointed to settle with the county of Nelson for levies paid before and after Hardin county was erected.

JULY TERM, 1794

Rosannah Swank administered upon the estate of her deceased husband, John Swank. John Swank lived in a fort of his own two miles northeast of Elizabethtown. He and his wife on a travel to Bardstown were waylaid and attacked by the Indians. Both of their horses were shot under them and Mrs. Swank was wounded in the arm. In attempting to make their escape after running a short distance her horse fell dead under her; she had a new saddle which she stripped from the dead animal and hung it in a tree. Swank's horse, being yet able to go, he dismounted and put his wife on his saddle, and he fled on foot to a cave on the old Cofer farm two miles from his fort. His dog betrayed him by barking at the pursuing Indians, and he was pierced by nineteen bullets and killed instantly.

Mrs. Swank fled on her husband's wounded horse until he failed. She left the dying horse and escaped on foot, and being a fleshy woman and clad in a new heavy linsey dress, she pulled it off as she ran, and so strong was her carefulness that she saved every pin and stuck them in an even row in the bosom of her dress.

She lived many years after, a skillful and popular midwife. Swank's fort occupied the ground where her son-in-law, William Edlin, afterwards lived and died. She left considerable family of Swank's, the most of whom became rich or comfortable and subsequently removed to

Missouri. The Edlin family now residing among us are the grandchildren.

CLERKS

At the July term, 1794, John Paul, who had been acting as clerk pro tem., produced a certificate of his qualification from the Judges of the Court of Appeals and was permanently made clerk of the County Court of Hardin.

August term, 1794, the court appointed commissioners to inspect the jail built by Isaac Larue and reported it well done, and allowed 12 pounds 16 shillings, equal to $42.66⅔. This was a cheap jail, although it was built of poplar round logs. It was standing within my recollection, but terribly bored by bumble bees—and never was worth a flint as a jail.

The next day the sheriff protested the public jail as insufficient.

October term, 1794, John Paul, clerk, was allowed 12 pounds 14 shillings for record book and traveling expenses on horseback to Lexington and back, ex-officio, services, paper, etc. Sheriff allowed 6 pounds 5 shillings for ex-officio services in 1793, and 8 shillings for a ticket box for the use of the election for that year, voting by ballot, I suppose.

COURT HOUSE TO BE LET

January term, 1795, Court held at the house of John Vertrees.

"Ordered that the Court House be let to the lowest bidder at the next March Court, agreeable to a plan that will be read on that day, and that the sheriff advertise the same."

Ichabod Radley was sworn as Deputy for Isaac Hynes, Sheriff. Ichabod Radley was a Down Easter, and had a better English education than common for that day, and was employed by William Hardin, of Hardin's settlement, as a teacher. The late Hon. Ben Hardin, Robert Wickliffe and many other men of note were his pupils. He was the first who shook the birch over my head. In passing through the Valley to Bardstown he became acquainted with Hannah Bush, daughter of the elder Christopher Bush; that acquaintance ripened into love and in due course of time they were married. They raised quite a family and all left the country but our fellow citizen, Isaac Radley, Esq., a gentleman of property in this town. He has filled the place of Deputy and high Sheriff several years and counted as an excellent officer, and now stands at the head of a genteel and worthy family.

THE COURT HOUSE ON WHEELS

The Court had fixed the place for erecting the Court House in the Valley; but the settlers around Hodgen's mill wanted it there, and in order to give every place a fair shake, the Court at March term, 1795, passed the following order verbatim, to-wit:

"Ordered that it be advertised that the Court have no objection to the public buildings of Hardin county being erected in any convenient place where the largest superscription may be made for; provided, a sufficient superscription may be made by the next May Court."

MAY TERM, 1795

Samuel Haycraft, gentleman, produced a commission from Governor Isaac Shelby, appointing him sheriff of Hardin county, and was qualified and gave bond with John Vertrees, Stephen Rawlings and John Paul, his securities.

Edward Rawlings was admitted and qualified as Deputy Sheriff.

SPUNKY DEPUTY SHERIFF

Edward Rawlings, son of Stephen, was then a young man, afterwards Captain Rawlings. He was a slender, tall man, with but little surplus flesh, nearly all muscle, very active, and prided himself on his manhood and high sense of chivalric honor. A warrant was placed in his hands to arrest "Bill Smothers," who was a rollicking kind of outlaw, and frequently guilty of personal outrages. He infested the lower end of the county—now Daviess county (which I omitted in my first number to set down as part of Hardin), about 130 miles from the present Court House. Rawlings, by strategem and some help, arrested Smothers, tied him on a horse and started with him on a long journey for the jail. When on the road between Hartford and Hardin's settlement, Smothers addressed Rawlings something after this manner:

"Ned, I have heard of you, and that you boast yourself to be much of a man. Is it fair if you are a better man than me? I promised to go with you untied, and if I prove to be the better man then let me go."

Rawlings was too high strung and chivalric to stand that, immediately dismounted and untied his prisoner, and at it they went.—and, like James Fitz James and Rhoderic Dhu, without a spectator to behold the contest, they were well matched. Their brawny arms encircled each other, and every power of muscle, sinew and bone was put in requisition and it would have afforded a rare chance for a special artist. The contest was long and doubtful. But Smothers, being as accustomed to hardships and lying in the woods as the wild beasts, outwinded the Deputy and came off the victor, and accordingly went his way, and Rawlings considered that the matter had been settled by the code of honor, fist and skull, and was content with the issue. His fee in case of success would have been three shillings in tobacco at a penny ha-penny per pound.

SUPERSCRIPTION FAILING—COURT HOUSE TO BE BUILT IN THE VALLEY

At May term, 1795, appears the following entry of record:

"At our last Court an order was passed to advertise that the Court had no objection to the public building being erected by superscription was brought forward at this Court, but no superscription appearing, the Court proceeded to let out the building of the Court House to the lowest bidder, which was cried off to John Crutcher, gentleman, at 66 pounds, to be built agreeable to a plan which was read at the Court House door. It is not exactly certain where the Court House door was, as there was no public Court House. Most likely it was at the door of Capt. John Vertrees, on the spot where James S. Howey now lives.

The Court adjourned till Court in course to be held in Elizabethtown.

This is the first time that the place was designated as Elizabethtown. It was thirty acres of land laid out by Col. Andrew Hynes in 1793 as a place to erect the public buildings, and at this time the name was given in honor of the Colonel's wife, Mrs. Elizabeth Hynes.

This action of the Court settled the point where the Court House should be, so far as the Court was concerned, but it was not satisfactory to the whole county, as it was only ten miles from the upper end of the county, and one hundred and thirty miles from the lower end of the county, which was sparsely settled.

The controversy was between the settlement of Nolin and the dwellers in the Valley. The Nolin settlements consisted chiefly of the

Hodgens, Larues, Phillipses, Kirkpatricks, Deremiahs, Ashcrafts, Dyes, Walters, Kostars, etc.

The Valley settlement was composed of the Helms, Hyneses, Churchills, Millers, Haycrafts, Bushes, Percifuls, Bruces, VanMeters, Shaws, Bruners, Bells, etc., the Valley being rather the most numerous.

There was hot blood all the time from 1794 to about 1803, each settlement believing they ought to have the county seat, and the controversy was bitter and hostile feelings divided the two sections. But particularly at the annual elections the feeling could not be controlled and during that period was the occasion of at least fifty combats of fist and skull, there being no pistols, knives, brass knucks or slungshots used in those days. The only unfair weapon used to my knowledge was by a young man by the name of Bruce, who had his shoes pointed with iron or steel, something like gaffs, being himself addicted to chicken fighting.

On one occasion, when quite small, I remember to have seen about twenty couple fighting at once at the end of Main Cross street, near where the bridge now stands. I think that was the last conflict. It terminated in a running skirmish as far out as the long hollow. But these matters have long since been forgotten, feelings and friendly relations having been restored.

Hodgenville is now the county seat of Larue county, which was struck off from Hardin in 1842 and is a flourishing, pleasant town.

CHAPTER V

COURT HOUSE BUILT AND A NEW COMER ON THE SAME DAY

The Court House must be built—John Crutcher, gentleman, was the undertaker for sixty-six pounds, equal to about $220, more or less. It was considered a pile—well it was to go up in the woods. The trees were all around. The old Kentucky axe with a good hand at the off-wheel, could fell the trees. The broadaxe could hew, the whipsaw could cut the plank, the frow and drawing-knife make the shingles (to be put on with wooden pegs), all to be had within one hundred yards of the spot. Uncle Johnny was a pusher, and he had willing hands—and such a ringing of the woodman's axe, such a crushing of falling trees, such a whizzing of the whipsaw as it ran up and down—by the job—by the job—in double quick. Then such a scoring and hewing, such a sawing and riving and snaving. Then the many songs and jibes of the laborers making vocal the grand forest—nothing equal to the excitement was experienced since Indian times.

Many hands made light work, so that on the 14th day of August, 1795, most glorious day, all was ready for the grand raising. Skids and hand-spikes and pushing dog-wood forks all ready, and forty strong hands on the ground with numerous women and children to behold the grand sight.

A little difficulty sprang up about the feeding of such a large force of healthy, hearty men, each of whom could lift three or four times as much weight, and each of them could eat nearly the tenth part of his weight avoirdupois.

My father's double log-house cabin was the only chance. The old house stood about seventy yards southeast of the fine dwelling house of T. H. Gunter, Esq. It was in the middle of what is now the railroad tract, and in this connection I will show what the women of the olden time could perform. My mother and eldest sister, with some younger ones, to hand things and bring water, got the dinner in the style of those halcyon days. Large loaves of bread from the clay oven, roast shoats, chickens, ducks, potatoes, roast beef with cabbage and beans, old-fashioned baked custard and pudding, and the indispensable pies, pickles, etc., etc.

Well, the dinner was set, all hands had their fill, the men back to their work, the table cleared off, the crumbs shook out to the dogs, the dishes, pewter spoons, knives, forks and pewter basins wiped and stowed away on the shelf of the dresser—that brought nearly 3 o'clock, p. m. On that remarkable occasion and about that time I made my first appearance on the stage of action, but as a new comer I was in a pitiable plight and destitute condition, for I was naked as a rat, without a cent of money and no pocket to put it in if I had a copper.

But I fell into good hands—was well clothed and fed, grew a little, and have weathered the storms of seventy-four winters and summers, having retained my eyesight, hearing, smelling, taste and appetite in a remarkable manner, and scandal says yet very fond of a good cup of coffee.

Thus far I have been somewhat tedious in giving the proceedings of a county court in olden times, omitting the innumerable stock marks, administrators, deeds acknowledged in open court, constable appointment, etc.

TOWN ESTABLISHED

At a court held on the fourth day of July, 1797.

PRESENT

Robert Hodgen, Stephen Rawlings and George Helm, gentlemen justices.

On motion of Andrew Hynes, Esq., who together with Benjamin Helm, his security, entered into and acknowledged their bond, conditioned agreeably to an act of assembly vesting the county courts with power to establish towns, etc. Whereas thirty acres of land, the property of the said Andrew Hynes, has been laid off in town lots, and the public buildings for the county of Hardin erected thereon, agreeable to the plan laid down and recorded in the Clerk's office. It is considered by the court that the town so laid off be established and known by the name of Elizabethtown. Ordered that the following persons be appointed trustees to said town, to-wit: Robert Hodgen, Benjamin Helm, Armstead Churchill, John Vertrees, Stephen Rawlings, Samuel Haycraft, Isaac Morrison and James Crutcher.

SECOND JAIL

At the same term, July, 1797, the repairing of the Court House and the erecting of stocks (whipping-post included) was let to Stephen Rawlings at 24 pounds; also the building of a new jail was sold to said Rawlings at 150 pounds, the work to be completed by the first day of January next.

This was a substantial hewed log building, lined with thick oak plank, spiked well with wrought spikes, and was built on the spot where the public well is now situated. In those days men were imprisoned for debt, a mistaken policy, a relic of hard times and barbarism long since exploded, and in course of a few years many men, white and black, were confined in the stocks and flogged at the whipping-post. The manner of punishment in the stocks was this: The offender was placed upon his knees, his head and hands placed through the holes formed in two planks, the upper one sliding in a groove, let down and fastened with a lock. If the man was dead drunk he was laid on his back and his feet inserted in two holes made to suit the case. He laid there until he was sober.

An old statute required a ducking stool for scolding women, but our old county court gentlemen were too gallant to avail themselves of that kind of machine, and let the fair sex scold on ad libitum if they chose.

The last described jail stood some years, and a man confined for debt concluded to burn his way out, fired the jail, and the jailer being out of the way, it was with much difficulty he was saved from being burned alive. The jail burned down, and the prisoner was indicted for arson, but was acquitted, and being a bricklayer, afterwards put up the best brick house in town, and in 1826 fell heir to an estate of $9,000 in England.

CLERK RESIGNED—HIS PLACE FILLED

On the 5th day of March, 1800, John Paul, clerk of the County Court, resigned his office, and Ben Helm, Esq., who produced a certificate of qualification, was appointed in the place of Paul. Major Helm held the office until February, 1817, when he resigned. Mr. Helm died in February, 1858. In the May following he would have been ninety-one years old.

Here I must anticipate the chronology of my history running out the jails and court house matters.

STONE JAIL

The building of a new jail (the third jail), to be of stone, was let to Charles Helm on the 25th day of November, 1806, at $2,485. The jail was to be forty-two feet long and twenty-one feet wide. The dungeon was under ground after the barbarous plan of old feudal times. The jail was divided so as to admit of the jailer residing in it. An example of this may be found more than 1,800 years ago, being authorized by the New Testament. I mean the jail at Phillippi, where Paul and Silas were confined in chains. Being devotional men, they sang praises to God and prayed at the dead hour of midnight. When the jail was shaken with an earthquake, the fetters fell off the prisoners, and the jailer sprang in and was about to slay himself, thinking his prisoners had escaped, but was told to do himself no harm, as they were all there.

Then the jailer, whose character has been often abused, proved himself to be a pretty clever fellow. My readers will please pardon this digression.

I think that the first jailer in that new prison was the Rev. Benjamin Ogden, a Methodist preacher. He was a chairmaker and a good workman in wood. He was the first Methodist preacher I ever saw. He came to Elizabethtown in 1803 or 1804, and his first effort was to raise a school. He came to my father's house on school business, and I well remember that I was terribly frightened when I heard that I was to go to his school, but on better acquaintance I learned to reverence and love him. He was a good man and a fair preacher. The next jailer was Frederick Tull, who died in the jail with the old cholera plague in 1814. Then followed Daniel Johnson, John Haywood and Enoch Lucky, who I believe was the last jailer in the stone house. Some years after the present brick jail was erected. It was undertaken and built by James Perceful. Richard May was the architect, and John Redman, blacksmith, framed the iron grates. I recollect that I was one of the commissioners to superintend the building, and after the wall was up a crack was discovered in the brickwork, and Perceful had to suffer a reduction of nearly a thousand dollars. But after standing some twenty years, in settling of the house, the crack closed up, and by the intercession of myself and the other commissioners the County Court made an allowance of five hundred dollars to Perceful and it was paid.

CHAPTER VI

On the 18th day of April, 1804, the building of the present brick Court House was let to James Perceful, and it was completed and received on the 22nd day of December, 1806. James Crutcher, Ben Helm, Robert Huston, Samuel Haycraft and John W. Holt, Esq., superintended the work. It was then considered to be a fine house, and the country flocked in to see it. Its fame spread far and wide—so much so that Butler County years afterward adopted the plan throughout in building their court house.

It still stands now in 1869, after having undergone many alterations and repairs, and is now decidedly the poorest and most uncomfortable court house in the State, considering the wealth and population of the county. But its old weather-beaten and rusty walls are entitled to some veneration on account of its past history of sixty-three years.

That house has been the theatre of some of the loftiest forensic displays. Its walls have reverberated the eloquence of the Hons. William McClung, John Rowan, Benjamin Hardin, John J. Crittenden, John Pope, Felix Grundy, Charles A. Wickliffe, John L. Helm, Thomas Chilton, Charles G. Wintersmith, Benjamin Tobin, Benjamin Chapeze and John Hays, of the old practitioners, all of whom except two are in their graves, and a host of other lawyers of more recent date, of whom it is my purpose to notice in proper time if my life is spared and health permits.

Eminent ministers of nearly all denominations have preached in it. A vast amount of eloquent breath has been blown in it by candidates for State and county offices. The clerk's offices were kept in it for several years. Schools have been taught in it. Public exhibitions and Indian dances in it were frequent. Many men have left it with the doom of death or penitentiary weighing upon them.

Our national jubilees were celebrated in it, parties and balls have been held in it, and the youth of our country, male and female, have tripped the light fantastic toe, and during the late civil war it was repeatedly occupied by armed soldiers.

So far I have been confined to the operations of the County Court, the erection of public buildings and other matters connected therewith, and thus ran ahead of the history.

I now will turn my attention to the Quarter Session and Circuit Courts held in Elizabethtown and in the woods before it was a town. Here endeth the first lesson on courts.

BACK TO THE WOODS AGAIN—QUARTER SESSION COURT

On the 26th day of February, 1793, the first Quarter Session Court (being the first court held in the county) was held in the house of Isaac Hynes in Severn's Valley.

A commission was produced appointing Phillip Phillips, Joseph Barnett and Thomas Helm, Justices of the Court of Quarter Sessions, who being sworn took their seats; and in the same commission Patrick Brown, John Vertrees, John Paul, William Hardin and Alexander

Barnett, gentlemen, were appointed Justices of the Hardin county court.

FIRST CLERK

Isaac Morrison was appointed clerk pro tempore.

FIRST SHERIFF

Isaac Hynes, Esq., produced a commission as sheriff of Hardin county, gave bond and qualified.

John Vertrees, Esq., was qualified as Justice of the Peace.

FIRST ATTORNEY

James Dohertie, gentleman, admitted to the bar as attorney at law and sworn, and the court adjourned.

This being the first term of court in Hardin county, a word or two about the Judges or Justices of the court may not be amiss. All three of them were Calvinistic Baptists. Hon. Judge Thomas Helm, the progenitor of all the Helms in the country, was from Virginia, and there ranked among the first families—and so held his rank here—was a gentleman in affluent circumstances, and lived and died where his fort was erected on the farm now owned by Mrs. Lucinda B. Helm, the estimable widow of the late Governor John L. Helm.

Hon. Judge Phillip Phillips was also a gentleman of large estate—lived on Nolin about ten miles from the Valley—was a man of much influence and figured for several years in Church and State to a considerable extent. Afterwards removed to Tennessee, where he died, leaving a large estate in lands and goods and chattles.

Hon. Judge Joseph Barnett was a Baptist preacher—lived near Hartford, and traveled upwards of seventy-five miles to sit in court. He possessed a large landed estate, and as before stated, was one of the preachers who constituted Severn's Valley Baptist Church, on the 17th day of June, 1781.

James Dohertie, Esq., who was first sworn attorney, came to the Valley a little in advance of the court, arriving at my father's on foot, without money and a perfect stranger. In order to make himself welcome to board and lodging assisted in making sugar, carrying water, heavy wood into the furnace and making himself generally useful. No person dreamed that he was a lawyer, and it produced no little astonishment when at the first court he pulled out his law license and was sworn in.

I have heard old pleople speak of Doherite as a prodigy in law knowledge, and a Boanerges in debates. But where he came from or where he went to, no mortal man now living can tell—it all happened before I was born. But gentlemen lawyers remember that James Dohertie was at the head of the bar in Hardin county before Elizabethtown had an existence.

APRIL TERM, 1793

Present Judges Phillip Phillips and Thomas Helm.

FIRST SUIT TRIED

Samuel and Christopher Bush against John Handley—attachment.

A jury found a verdict for nine pounds and five shillings and costs.

A little explanation may be necessary to show why an attachment was taken out against John Handley.

He had by some means got into a difficulty at Bardstown with John Gilpin, which ended in his killing Gilpin, and such was the dread and horror of killing a man in those days, that he fled until men had time to cool—the Bushes and others thought Handley never would return. He afterwards gave himself up, was tried and acquitted. He afterwards laid off the town of Vienna at the falls of Green River and lived many years, possessed of a handsome estate, and having occupied a high position in society, died at a good old age. One of his sons, George Handley, Esq., now of Larue county, was for years clerk of Davies county, and although an excellent clerk, voluntarily resigned the office and became a quiet gentleman farmer near the town of Hodgenville. Eight suits were disposed of at this term.

THIRD TERM, JUNE 25TH, 1793

A grand jury was impaneled and sworn, but such quiet and good order prevailed in the county that they had nothing to present—were discharged.

Banner Friend produced a commission and qualified as surveyor of Hardin county. John Paul, Robert Baird, Ben Helm and David Phillips, gentlemen, were sworn and admitted as deputy surveyors. Robert Hodgen, gentleman, sworn as Justice of the Peace.

It appears that the Quarter Session Court and County Court had or at least practiced concurrent jurisdiction. Deeds were acknowledged before each court, and each clerk recorded deeds until the establishment of the Circuit Court, then the County Court did all that business: sheriffs, surveyors, &c., were qualified in each court and so were justice of the peace.

Robert Hodgen, who was qualified at this term as a justice of the peace was from Virginia. He was an honorable high-toned gentleman of the good old school; was the soul of hospitality, and was well patronized in that line—was an active enterprising business man, and figured largely during life in the interest of the county and in the Baptist Church, of which he was counted a pillar. Two of his sons were preachers of the Gospel. His oldest son, Isaac Hodgen, was one of the best and most eloquent preachers of Kentucky. He was a man of large stature, and according to my notion was one of the finest looking men in the State.

His fine commanding presence, the great compass of his voice, which although music itself, was so powerful as to be distinctly heard a great distance; which, joined with his eloquence and logical reasoning and persuasive style, made him almost irresistible, insomuch that his labors were sought for at great distances. He was the founder of a church in Nashville, Tennessee, and afterwards sent as a delegate to the triennial convention of Baptists in the city of Philadelphia.

He died in Green county in the full vigor of life, and was supposed to have been poisoned.

Robert Hodgen died in 1809 or 1810 and left a large family. Of some of his descendants I may hereafter have occasion to speak in connection with the interests of Elizabethtown.

CHAPTER VII

SEPTEMBER TERM, 1793

Present—Phillip Phillips, Joseph Barnett and Thomas Helm, Justices.

William McClung and Sephen Ormsby, Esqs., were sworn and admitted to the bar as attorneys.

William McClung, Esq., was appointed Commonwealth's Attorney for this court.

Commonwealth's Attorneys were not then commissioned by the Governor—each county appointed their own prosecuting attorney—and were paid out of the county levy.

Stephen Ormsby was a native of Ireland, raised in Louisville, and was afterward Judge of the Hardin Circuit Court.

The first presentment of the Grand Jury was against Isaac Hynes, the Sheriff, for swearing.

TEMPORARY JAIL

The court made this order:

"Ordered that Isaac Hynes' still-house be appointed a temporary jail."

Isaac Hynes, gentleman, sheriff enters his protest against the sufficiency of the jail appointed by the court.

Isaac knew all about his own still-house and thought that it was sufficient so long as a prisoner was kept under the influence of his still-worm, but that under sober second thought, the prisoner could find egress at the door, or the window, or clab-bord roof, and therefore protested.

A new grand jury was impaneled who, seeming to get the hang of things, presented three different persons for retailing spiritous liquors without license—one was against the high sheriff, but the presentment against the sheriff was quashed on the ground that he was a regular distiller.

The grand jury thus showing a laudable purpose to suppress vice and maintain the dignity of the law, were adjourned over to second day.

SECOND DAY

The grand jury again assembled and retired to the woods (as they had no room), and after due deliberation returned a batch of presentments for almost every conceivable minor offence, such as swearing, getting drunk, fighting and last, though not least, against two unmarried women for having children without the necessary appendage of a husband.

The court did not think that being a distiller authorized a man to swear as well as sell liquor and therefore ordered Isaac to add five shillings to the public funds.

DECEMBER TERM, 1794

James Nourse sworn as attorney at law.

FEBRUARY TERM, 1795—CLERK PRO TEM HASTENED

Isaac Morrison having been appointed as clerk pro tempore from February term 1793, was ordered to produce a certificate of qualification by the next term or walk the plank.

The court took cognizance of the fact, that its terms had been held in the house of Isaac Hynes for two years past, to his great inconvenience, and allowed him ten pounds and directed the county to pay him.

APRIL TERM, 1795—A NEW CLERK PRO TEMPORE

Isaac Morrison, the clerk pro tem., not producing a certificate of qualification the court appointed David May clerk pro tem. Court sat three days.

JUNE TERM, 1795

Present—Thomas Helm and John Carnahan, Judges.

Richard Dickerson sworn as attorney at law.

Quite a batch of presentments at this term for profane swearing, getting drunk, fighting; also, against a man and woman for living together without the sanction of a priest.

Also, a presentment against Ben. Parker for threatening the life of Christopher Bush, also for being a general disturber of the peace. Bush was then and for many years a constable, and being a man of determination, was a great interruption to such men as Parker. Litigation having increased the court sat for four days.

SEPTEMBER TERM

Hon. Felix Grundy admitted as attorney at law.

From the presentments at this term it appears that swearing profanely and getting drunk had greatly increased—wolves were numerous in the county and whole flocks of sheep were destroyed.

The grand jury in a presentment petitioned the Legislature to declare wolves outlaws, and fix a price on their scalps.

DECEMBER TERM, 1795

Allen Milton Wakefield, Esq., was admitted as attorney at law. I know but little of his history; he was one of the first Judges appointed under the Circuit Court system in 1803.

FEBRUARY TERM, 1796

Present—Judges Thomas Helm, John Carnahan and John Vertrees.

Captain Vertrees on that day produced his commission as Quarter Session Justice.

Hon. John Pope sworn as attorney at law.

FIRST CAPITAL PUNISHMENT IN THE COUNTRY

Jacob, a negro slave, the property of John Crow, killed his master on the 30th day of December, 1795. They were both cutting on the same fallen tree—the negro at the butt end, the master high up. Crow thinking that Jacob was not working with a will, came to inspect Jacob's cut, reproved him for sloth and turned away to resume his chopping; as soon as his back was turned Jacob dealt him a blow in the head with his axe, which killed him outright. Jacob drew his dead master to the side of an old log and covered him with leaves.

He then fled to Vienna at the falls of Green River. As soon as the murder was discovered, Phillip Taylor pursued and took Jacob. When arrested he said to Taylor, "I killed Crow, but you prove it." The prisoner was conveyed in a canoe to the mouth of Rough Creek, and up Rough Creek to Hartford, and from thence was brought under guard to Elizabethtown in the Valley.

On the second day of March, 1796, by consent of the prisoner, he was tried by a called court, composed of Judges Thomas Helm and John Vertrees. On arrangement Jacob pleaded guilty, and he was sentenced to be hung by the neck until he was dead, dead, dead, and the Lord is invoked to have mercy on him, and the sheriff, Samuel Haycraft, was ordered to carry the sentence into execution on the second day of April, 1796, between the hours of twelve and two o'clock.

The court not agreeing on the value of the negro, a jury was impaneled who fixed his value at eighty pounds.

As murder at that day was of rare occurrence and this perhaps the first in the county, it produced quite a sensation, and particularly so, as John Crow was a man of some note and highly esteemed.

The prisoner was confined in the old poplar log jail and there being no jailor, the sheriff with a guard was charged with the custody of Jacob. A few days before the execution, the sheriff being absent, the duty of feeding the prisoner devolved on my mother. On opening the door to hand in his dinner, the prisoner made a desperate dash, upset the old lady and ran for life. The Hon. George Helm, the father of Gov. Helm, being in sight, and being then a stout young man, pursued the prisoner about four hundred yards, crossing Valley creek and ascending a hill, caught and brought him back. He was then kept safely until the day fixed for his execution, the 2nd day of April, 1796.

As is usual to this day, on such occasions, the execution was witnessed by a vast crowd.

The sheriff having a distaste for the hangman's office (by consent of Jacob) procured the services of a black man to tie the noose and drive the cart from under.

The writer was less than a year old, and I suppose was not there but for years afterwards he heard the matter spoken of as an era in time, "The time Jacob was hung."

APRIL TERM, 1796

Present—Thomas Helm, John Carnahan and John Vertrees.

I will here note that quarter session courts had the same jurisdiction that circuit courts now have, and that the presiding officers were really Judges, and entitled to that honorable appellation, but like Judges of the United States Court were styled Justices.

At this term Henry Power Brodnax and David Donan, Esqs., were sworn and admitted as attorneys.

I have no recollection of Donan; Brodnax afterwards became a Circuit Judge; he lived and died a bachelor, was scrupulously neat, wore short breeches with white stockings, knee and shoe buckles of silver and kept everything in print; was polite and attentive to the fair sex, and was urgent in his advice to them not to suffer a wrinkle in their stockings. On the bench he was a terror to evil doers—very strict in this discipline of the court. He was in the habit of breaking in a new sheriff and for a few terms ruled over him as with a rod of iron; but as soon as he imagined that the sheriff had fallen into traces, he began to treat him as a gentleman. In the latter part of his life he professed religion and united with the Cumberland Presbyterian church, and was remarkable as a very zealous member of that zealous body of Christians. He then commenced wearing long pants and became a little more careless in his dress. Although he had a farm near Russellville, he boarded at a hotel in that city many years. He had a servant man named Brandy, who was major domo, and was a great favorite of the Judge's and attended to the dairy, which furnished better butter than was to be found anywhere else.

I visited his room at the Edwards Hotel in 1817. It was fitted up to his own notion, and had whole shelves of the finest cordials, manufactured by himself with the assistance of his man Brandy. These delicacies were more for his friends than for his own use, as he was quite a temperance man. He was a remarkable man, of the strictest integrity, somewhat eccentric, and when off the bench, of social and genial habits.

After 1818 I lost sight of him, living one hundred miles apart.

CHAPTER VIII

ATTORNEYS' FEES MADE SAFE—APRIL TERM, 1796

It was ruled by the Court that if a person presented by the grand jury should confess himself guilty of the foul deed and pay the fine, it should not hinder the attorney from pocketing his fee.

PUBLICATION VS. NON-RESIDENCE—HICKMAN VS. TOBIN

Order of publication in the Kentucky Gazette, and also to be published at the door of Captain John Vertrees, a place of public worship immediately after divine service.

This is the first notice of a place of public worship I can find of an official character in the county.

A friend has suggested that anybody would know I was a Baptist after reading my second number. By way of explanation I here state that the Baptists were the pioneers of the Valley, and that no other orthodox denomination had a representation on these waters for many years after. Subsequently other denominations of good Christians came and organized churches that were prosperous and did much good in the cause of religion. And of those churches I propose to make honorable mention at the proper dates.

HIGH-BLOODED FEES AT THE TERM, APRIL, 1796

Alexander Barnett, Justice of the Peace, was fined £5 and the costs for charging Christopher Jackson high-blooded fees for official services.

PERMANENT CLERK

David May, who had been acting as clerk pro tem., produced a certificate of his qualifications, was permanently appointed clerk and gave bond. His son, Samuel May, was sworn in as deputy. The term of the court was continued five days.

ISAAC HYNES

Previous to this time and from the beginning of the county, frequent mention has been made of the name of Isaac Hynes. The courts had been held in his house for more than two years. He was sheriff, and had a still house, which on one occasion was made a temporary jail, and against the sufficiency of which Isaac protested for reasons stated in my seventh chapter.

He was in the habit of swearing, almost equal to Uncle Toby's army in Flanders, and of which the grand juries frequently made honorable mention, and by way of a change in his amusements now and then took a chunk of a fight. When I knew him he was a square-built man of middle age with a sprinkle of gray hairs—was considered rather beforehand in the world, always had money and was looked upon as quite a character in his day, had many friends and a few enemies. But how, when or where he wound up this deponent, not knowing, saith not, and I suppose there is not a white man living who could tell.

There is one man in this town older than myself. His name is Charles Slaughter, a colored man, aged ninety-three years. I asked him what became of Isaac Hynes and he does not know. But as Charles Slaughter is a deserving man, sixty-seven years a member of the church, I expect to take notice of him in due time.

SEPTEMBER TERM, 1796

At this time the population had increased—the rich soil abundantly repaid the husbandman for his toil and plenty filled the land, and, true to the character of Old Virginia, the mother State, the inhabitants set no bounds to their hospitality. About this time my father erected a new house with a basement and two high stories upon it, with a stone chimney, which took more than one hundred wagon loads to build it. It was considered then rather aristocratic. The large yellow poplar timbers of which it was erected are sound to this day—1869.

The court at this term directed Robert Hodgen to issue a summons against Robert Jackson, presented by the grand jury as coming under the vagrant law, and deal with him as the law directs. The law directed such gentry upon conviction to be sold for twelve months to the highest bidder, and from my knowledge of the Squire charged with this service, I have no doubt that Jackson was cried off at public sale. But as such plenty abounded, a few attempted to get a living by vagabondizing.

But to return to the new house. I do not remember the year, but it was when I was about ten years old, that remarkable day called cold Friday, rolled up in the calendar, no person before or since experienced such a day—clear as a bell and cold as Canada; the air was filled with glistening, sparkling flakes of frost; cows froze to death. On that day my younger brother, Roads Vanmeter and myself were set to beat a mess of hominy in the basement, being the cooking department, with a fireplace nearly seven feet wide, with a large fire in it. Neither of us being overly fond of work, we scrupulously divided the work with an iron wedge inserted in a pestle. One hundred licks each in turn was administered to the corn in the mortar, occasionally pouring in hot water to excelerate the work, but the water almost instantly froze and the wedge sent back the sound chow, chow, chow, the whole being a frozen mass. At night we had no impression upon the corn and the work was adjourned over.

The next day we cut out the frozen corn, put it in a pot over a hot fire and gave it two honest hours' boiling, then put it in the mortar and finished the work; this completed, the trio formed themselves into a drum-head courtmartial to try the inventor of hominy beating, and the sentence was unanimous that the inventor ought to be hung. Neither of us ate of that hominy.

Perhaps this recital may appear trival, but it has hung upon my memory for sixty-four years, and I thought I might as well record it as a matter of history and let it cease to be a matter of tradition.

AT THIS SAME TERM, SEPTEMBER, 1789

From the records at this term it appears that some Spanish prisoners had been on hand and a considerable expense was incurred in guarding, handcuffing and taking them to Logan jail, but all the witnesses are dead. I am not able to state the cause of the arrest.

I have some vague recollection of mule loads of gold being distributed among some high officials in some way connected with the Spanish territory of which Missouri was a part.

At this term a case came up for a breach of peace—James Nourse and Felix Grunday were attorneys for plaintiff and Rowan for defendant. The name of John Rowan appeared several times on record before this, but I have not been able to find where he was admitted to the bar. More of him hereafter.

TAKING TIME BY THE FORELOCK—OCTOBER TERM, 1797

The court appointed Samuel May clerk pro tempore, provided David May, the present clerk, departed this life.

I would here note that David May was a highly esteemed gentleman and was the progenitor of all the Mays of this county.

Hon. Joseph Barnett, having departed this life leaving an immense estate in lands, and his children being minors, the legislature of Kentucky, by a strange enactment, appointed Gen. Stephen Cleaver, Henry Rhodes and Harrison Taylor commissioners to manage and settle the estate.

At this term in the case of Joseph Barnett's commissioners against Robert Baird, the court appointed Henry P. Brodnax, John Rowan, Felix Grunday, Newman Edwards, John Pope and Gabriel Johnson, or any three of these arbitrators in the case, and their award to be made the judgment of the court.

All of these arbitrators were practicing lawyers in the Hardin Quarter Session Court. Their history is too well known to make it necessary to say that they were distinguished men. But I will say that such a galaxy of eminent men were hardly ever before charged with such a case of private controversy. Either of these men was far ahead in legal knowledge, statesmanship and administrative capacity of some of our Presidents. In giving a history of the bar I shall have occasion to speak of them more in detail. Three of them were afterward judges of the Court of Appeals, one a circuit judge, one a minister to Mexico, two of them were senators in Congress, and one of them a member of Congress and one a governor.

CHAPTER IX

In my last chapter I had occasion to mention the commissioners of Joseph Barnett's estate.

Many years after the reference of the case of Barnett's commissioners against Baird, while at Frankfort I was much amused in reading a petition of Joseph Barnett, Jr. (son of the deceased), to the Legislature, in which he set out in his peculiar sarcastic style: That his father had died "possessed of an estate in lands sufficient to set two tyrants at war and his children all of tender years. And the Legislature had undertaken to be guardians for the children, and their agents had appointed three men as commissioners to manage and settle the estate; that these commissioners, while they were not dishonest, were too ignorant to be honest.

"That the harpies, taking advantage of their want of business capacity, had hovered around, feasted, gorged and fattened themselves on the spoil, and that the bungling of the commissioners had frittered the estate away. That he wanted no more Legislature enactments on the subject, but just to stand out of his moonshine while he carried into Grant the numerous entries and surveys of land made by Joseph Barnett, now deceased."

The commissioners were all honest men, but lacked business qualifications; without any disrespect to the memory of Harrison Taylor, for he was a good man, but claimed the right to have a dictionary of his own, and had as much right as Walker, Webster or Johnson to teach spelling. On one occasion he wrote to his merchant to send him a specific quantity of KAUGHPHY, managing in his orthography to spell the word with the complete sound, without using a solitary letter with which our bungling merchants were accustomed to spell, and who knows but that he was right, and that spelling it COFFEE is an arbitrary usage.

In legal terms he also had his way; wanting a process to compel the production of a paper, which process our lawyers term subpœna duces tecum, he applied for missile with a sharper edge, a writ of axim stickma.

CLERKS RAPIDLY MADE AT FEBRUARY TERM, 1798

David May, the clerk, having departed this life, the court appointed John Helm to fill the vacancy, and he gave bond, with William McClung and George Helm as his securities, in the penalty of $3,000. George Helm produced a commission as sheriff and was ordered to qualify at the next term. On motion of John Helm, clerk, Maurice Miles was admitted as his deputy. Court adjourned 2nd day of the term. John Helm, who was appointed clerk on yesterday, resigned his office. Maurice Miles was appointed clerk and gave bond, with Felix Grundy and John Rowen as securities; penalty, $3,000. Maurice Miles was a business man of fine promise, wrote a beautiful business hand, and would have made an excellent clerk, but he lived but a short time.

Of John Helm, who held the office of clerk but one day, I propose in my next number to give an extended account, as having acted a prominent part in the thrilling events of the early settlement of the Valley.

FIRST PRESS FOR PUBLIC PAPERS

At the same term, February, 1798:

"Ordered, That the clerk of this court employ a fit person to make a press for the public papers, at the public expense, and make a report to this court."

That press was made of walnut wood, and was the only press in the office when I entered as deputy in 1809.

The papers up to this time, say six years, had been kept in a basket and bread tray. The orders of court had previously been simply short minutes, and the greater part of the judgments were so indefinite that it required a reference to the papers of the suits to ascertain the amounts recorded. Even in the celebrated case of Barnett's commissioners against Baird, which had been referred to such eminent lawyers as arbitrators, a note was made by the clerk that an award was returned and that award was made the judgment of the court.

But what that award was, after an intimate acquaintance with the office for nearly sixty years, I have never been able to learn, nor is there a man above ground that can tell.

APRIL TERM, 1798

At this time Henry P. Brodnax produced a license and was sworn as attorney-at-law.

(Note.—He had been previously sworn and admitted to the bar; perhaps he had been admitted before on the militia system, without license. I have spoken of him at length in my seventh chapter.)

Richard Harris, Esq., produced a license and was sworn as attorney-at-law.

The grand jury had little to do at this term, as appears by the following entry:

"The grand jury returned into court and made the following presentment: 'We present Samuel Forrester for profane swearing (By God),' and having nothing further to present, were discharged."

This term lasted four days. The heaviest part of the docket was for and against Joseph Barnett's commissioners.

The winding up of the term was an order authorizing the Commonwealth's Attorney to proceed legally, by information or otherwise, against John Lawson Hall for arson, in burning the house of Joseph Greenawalt, the court being of the opinion that the evidence was strong against him, and to make things secure Hall was bound over to keep the peace on the complaint of Nellie Greenawalt, the wife of Joseph.

JUNE TERM, 1798

The grand jury presented a woman for having a child without the aid of a legal husband, deeming such proceeding a little out of order.

The court directed George Berry, Esq., J. P., to pay attention to this little affair.

The most specific entry of a judgment was at this term as follows:

"Vanmetre vs. Sharp—judgment confessed for £25 with interest from 7th, 1796—(fee paid) and cost."

Another not so definite as to interest:

"Marshall vs. Parepoint—issue waived, judgment confessed for £10 with interest from day it became due till paid, reserving equity."

JUNE TERM, 1799

James Crutcher, Esq., produced commission as quarter session justice from James Garrard, governor, was sworn and took his seat.

Maurice Miles, the clerk of this court, having departed this life, Major Ben Helm was appointed clerk pro tempore and gave bond, with John Rowan and Felix Grundy his sureties—penalty, $3,000.

James Nourse, Esq., attorney for the Commonwealth, having departed this life, his administrators were allowed £15 for the year 1799.

APRIL TERM, 1800

Samuel Brunts, Esq., was appointed and sworn as Commonwealth's Attorney pro tempore.

Brunts, who afterward corrected the spelling of the family name to Brents, most likely the proper name, was sworn in several terms back, was an eminent lawyer, lived in Greensburg, and was afterward a member of the State Legislature, and afterward died in Greensburg of cholera in 1832 or 33.

MARCH TERM, 1802

Samuel Haycraft produced commission and took his seat as quarter session justice.

Robert Wickliffe and John W. Holt, Esqs., sworn as attorneys.

SEPTEMBER TERM, 1805

Nathaniel Wickliffe sworn as deputy clerk.

The record of the court's proceeding at this term were not signed by the judge.

REMARKS

Fearing that my readers have become wearied with the dull routine of court business, which has been given perhaps at the expense of patience of the reading public as rather prolix and ceased to be interesting, I will omit them in the future, and remark that the proceedings of the courts up to the conclusion of September, 1802, were occasionally signed by the Rev. Judge Joseph Barnett and Judge Vertrees, but the great majority of the signatures was by the venerable Judge Thomas Helm, who appears to have been present at every term.

The old system of summoning jurors from the bystanders and running down men then existed, and they got no pay; and it was usual when the judges directed the sheriff to summon a jury that the court house was cleared in short order, and men might be seen, as if running for life, and the tails of their coats and hunting shirts sailing behind as they broke to the brush and tall grass, where they sometimes fell into yellow jackets' nests.

Perhaps as good an illustration of the jury system then in vogue as could be given occurred in the early courts of Indiana, perhaps out of my bounds, but it will bring up the thing naked.

In a round log cabin for a court house, with a pole across, dividing his honor from the masses of the people, the judge asked the sheriff if he had a jury ready. The sheriff replied that he had eleven tied up in the loft, and that the deputy was running down the twelfth.

Witnesses were allowed two shillings and sixpence per day and were not very apt to attend punctually, and many were summoned and fined for non-attendance.

The clerk kept no witness book up to this time, 1802, but their attendance was noted in the proceedings of the court.

Here endeth the second lesson on courts, being the death of the quarter session court system.

CHAPTER X

In my last chapter I promised to speak of John Helm, who was appointed clerk and resigned the office after holding it one day. He was born on 26th of November, 1761, in Prince William county, Virginia, and was the eldest son of Judge Thomas Helm, frequently spoken of in this history. His father landed on the Falls of the Ohio, near Louisville, in March, 1780, and at the close of the year removed to the Valley and built a fort. John Helm at nineteen years of age came to Kentucky, one year before his father's removal from Virginia. For those times he was well educated for a practical surveyor. He was of small stature, and not remarkable for strength or activity, the qualities that most adorned the forest gentleman of that day; but possessing a firm constitution, with great steadiness of purpose and habits, he was enabled to perform the most astonishing labor and to endure the greatest sufferings.

The qualities of his mind were well suited to his business, possessing in a superior degree a sound and discriminating judgment, united with patient and untiring investigation, and moral courage.

On reaching Kentucky he immediately commenced the dangerous occupation of locating and surveying lands, for which he had been educated.

His first trip was perhaps his most unfortunate, and as I cannot go into a detail of all, I will notice this and pass on. Having formed the usual company for surveys in those times, he commenced operations not far from the mouth of Salt River, accompanied by William Johnston, the father of the late Dr. Johnston, of the city of Louisville, for whom he was then surveying, a company of Indians having discovered them, and knowing their business, waylaid them while in the active employment of running a line. The Indians squatting in the small cane, through which they had to pass, as they came up fired, and rising up at the same moment, rushed upon them with their usual terrible yell. Mr. Helm being a little in advance, was in the midst of the Indians at the moment of the attack. The Indians, thinking him their captive, turned their attention to those in the rear. He used the fortunate moment, and passing through them made his escape. The others were killed or taken prisoners. Among the latter was William Johnston, and Helm alone remained to tell that all was lost.

Soon, another set of instruments being procured and the necessary arrangements made, young Helm again commenced the hazardous occupation, experience having taught him the necessity of caution in all his movements. The theater upon which he acted being generally between green and Salt rivers, many were the trials and sufferings through which he passed. The hairbreadth escapes and thrilling incidents of living in a constant state of warfare, sometimes driven from their work by the Indians, and at other times suffering from fatigue, cold and want of food; sometimes in assisting to defend his father's fort when attacked by the Indians, which was often the case; at other times venturing to the assistance of some neighboring fort, often forming one of a little band of volunteers to drive off a maraudering gang of Indians who were committing depredations upon the neighborhood.

Yet scenes of blood and strife will become familiar, and in the midst of them there will be marrying and giving in marriage. On the 22nd of

March, 1787, young Helm was married to Miss Sallie Brown, in Haycraft's fort, in the same neighborhood. In 1791 he went out in St. Clair's campaigns as a common soldier. But his capacity for business and superior education, more uncommon in those days than at present, could not long be overlooked. He performed all or nearly all the duties appertaining to the officers in Colonel Oldham's regiment of Kentucky militia, which formed one division of St. Clair's army. The regular troops formed the other division. Colonel Oldham and Mr. Helm being connected by marriage (Helm's mother being a Pope and Colonel Oldham's wife being a Pope) as well as by official relationship in the army, were on the most intimate terms and fully in each other's secrets. They were greatly dissatisfied with St. Clair's disposition of the army the night before the fatal battle. Oldham remonstrated with St. Clair and told him of the danger before him, but to no effect, and finally parted with him the evening before the battle with the prophetic warning that history would have to record the tale of sorrow which would be the result of blunders then making. Neither Oldham nor any of his principal officers slept that night. A little before day Mr. Helm was sent on a trip of discovery beyond the lines of the army, and while he was on this service the attack was commenced, the Indians rushing upon Oldham's division, which was about half a mile in advance of the main army, a small river or large creek between them.

Mr. Helm, taking a circuitous route, reached the ford and waded over with the retreating division. Immediately after crossing the river he met with Colonel Oldham, and while in conversation about the best course to pursue Colonel Oldham received a ball, passing through his body, and he fell. The Indians being in hot pursuit and near at hand, Helm could only stay a moment to receive the Colonel's dying message to his wife.

As history records all the particulars of this bloody scene, my purpose is only to speak of Mr. Helm as one of the actors on that occasion.

Assisted by the officers of the Kentucky division, he made every exertion to ward off the dreadful horrors of that day by trying to keep the way clear so that the army could retreat in some sort of order. They continued their exertions till scarcely one was left who was not dying or wounded.

Mr. Helm, while in the act of touching the trigger to shoot an Indian who was doing great mischief, received a ball in his left arm, shattering one of the bones from the wrist to the elbow. Thus disabled, he fell back among the wounded and dying, and for some time saw the efforts to regain possession of that point which he and his comrades had struggled so hard to hold. But St. Clair had committed the second great blunder and streams of blood had to be poured out before that important point was again obtained.

Some of the best and bravest officers of the Regular Army fell here, and several unsuccessful charges were made to no effect. By this time rain and death engulfed the army all around; no place was safe, the wounded often receiving the second and more fatal shot where they lay. Mr. Helm had no less than seven bullets passing through his clothes.

Seeing death or escape the only alternative and being surrounded by the enemy on every side, Major Patrick Brown, Captain Thomas (since General Thomas), Stephen Cleaver (since General Cleaver), Mr. Helm and a few others concluded to make a last desperate attempt to open a passage through the Indian lines, the only possible way by which to retreat. The Indians were doubly prepared, having twice resisted charges made by a division of the regular soldiers, but these men thought it was nothing but death any way and determined to make a trial for life. Their plans being settled, they called long and loud for Kentuckians to make a rush for home. That word home had a talismanic effect. Their young wives and little children shot up before the mind's eye and nerved them for the struggle, and with a desperate shout they charged the Indians without firing a gun. The Indians for a moment seemed to be panic stricken, yielded for them to pass, whilst the balance of the shattered army, as if by one impulse, followed after.

Mr. Helm, with the feelings and true spirit of a back woodsman, clung to his rifle—that treasure to be parted with only in death, his arm-bone broken and shattered as before mentioned—carrying his rifle, ran and marched with the army upwards of thirty miles that day. The sufferings from such a wound would have been great under the most favorable circumstances and best treatment, but awful indeed must they have been in a wilderness, with such treatment and accommodations as could be given in a retreating and defeated army, yet after months of suffering Helm returned to his family and was restored to health.

This closed the Indian fighting and he again resumed his occupation as surveyor. The Indians were no longer regarded as an object of dread and terror. The balance of his life was spent in active and useful labor, mostly as surveyor. He acted as county surveyor many years in Washington county, where he removed, and was associate judge in that county under the old system, and was a neat and thrifty farmer. He afterward removed to Breckinridge county and there farmed extensively, and finally removed to Elizabethtown. He had no political aspirations; although often urged, he never was a candidate for office before the people. He accumulated a considerable fortune, considering the theater upon which he acted and the county in which he lived; for these things are comparative, at least, yet few men ever came as near living and dying without an enemy. He died at his residence in Elizabethtown on the 3rd day of April, 1840, having been a faithful member of the Methodist Episcopal Church for seven years.

The foregoing notice of the Hon. John Helm is principally taken from his memoir (not only as to facts but nearly as to language), written in 1840 by his son, the Hon. B. Helm, now of Hannibal, Missouri.

CHAPTER XI

QUARTER SESSION AND DISTRICT COURTS ABOLISHED AND CIRCUIT COURTS ESTABLISHED

On the 20th day of December, 1802, the Legislature abolished the quarter session courts; on the 21st of the same month an amendment was made, by which the district courts were established.

A circuit court to be held in each county, to be composed of one circuit judge and two assistant judges. Nine judges were commissioned by the governor, by and with the consent of the Senate, for the State at large. Those judges, at a general court assembled at Frankfort, the capital, on the 4th Monday in January, 1803; and allotted to each judge his circuit and by allotment, the Hon. Stephen Ormsby was to preside in the counties of Nelson, Jefferson, Bullitt and Hardin. This allotment was given under the hands and seals of the following judges:

Samuel McDowell, John Colburn, B. Thurston, Stephen Ormsby, James G. Hunter, John Allen, Christopher Greenup and Allen Milton Wakefield.

HARDIN CIRCUIT COURT

On the 18th day of April, 1803, the Hon. Stephen Ormsby, circuit judge, and the Hon. Samuel Haycraft, and William Munford, assistant judges, organized the first circuit court in Elizabethtown.

CLERK APPOINTED

Major Ben Helm, who produced a certificate of qualification from under the hands and seals of the Hons. George Muter, Benjamin Sebastian and Caleb Wallace, judges of the Court of Appeals, was appointed clerk and gave bond, with Felix Grundy and Robert Wickliffe as securities.

The assistant judges were sworn before Asa Combs, Esq., justice of the peace and tavern keeper.

Alexander Pope, Esq., by consent of the court, undertook to prosecute as county attorney.

Felix Grundy, John W. Holt, Robert Wickliffe and Alexander Pope sworn and admitted as attorneys-at-law.

Nathaniel Wickliffe sworn as deputy clerk.

RULE DAYS

were appointed to be held in the clerk's office on Saturday after the 3rd Monday in each month. The object of rule days was intended for parties to prepare for trial and to file with the clerk their answers, pleas, republications, etc. The clerk kept a docket for that purpose, and when both parties were ready, cocked and primed, their cases were transferred to a trial of reference docket, then the case came before the court and jury, and many men then had to experience the glorious uncertainty of the law, the winners always admitting that a Daniel had come to judgment, and the losers asseverating that they were the victims of the blindness and superstition of fellow man, and although the rule docket has long since been dispensed with, yet the return days of executions in the Hardin Circuit Court has been the same days for sixty years to 1869.

The clerk was authorized to issue executions on all judgments of the quarter session courts now defunct. Having thus organized, the court adjourned until the next day at 7 o'clock a. m., at which time they met, examined and signed the orders and adjourned.

(Signed) STEPHEN ORMSBY.

JULY TERM, 1803—A NEW JUDGE

The general court having made a new allotment of circuits, the Hon. Christopher Greenup was allotted to the counties of Henry, Hardin, Livingston and Ohio.

This allotment signed by the same judges, with the addition of the name of the Hon. Ninian Edwards.

PRESENT

Hon. Christopher Greenup, circuit judge, and Samuel Haycraft, assistant judge.

David Trimble sworn as attorney-at-law.

SECOND DAY

H. P. Brodnax sworn as attorney-at-law.

This term lasted six days—each day's business signed

CHRISTOPHER GREENUP.

OCTOBER TERM, 1803

Present—Hon. Samuel Haycraft and William Munford.

The clerk recorded all the indictments in the order book—rather tedious.

SECOND DAY

Present also, Hon. Christopher Greenup, judge.

APRIL TERM, 1804—CIRCUIT CHANGED

Hon. Christopher Greenup allotted to the counties of Henry, Hardin, Muhlenburg and Ohio.

COMMONWEALTH
vs.
F. PAREPOINT. } On indictment of murdering Robert Kennedy.

Parepoint surrendered himself; was put upon trial and found not guilty.

The circumstances were: Parepoint had a process to arrest Kennedy on a penal charge. Kennedy and his wife were attending preaching at the old Baptist meeting house on the hill, where Mr. I. Robin Jacob now resides. Kennedy was ordered to stand, but chose to run, was shot in the back and died next day, and was buried in Vertrees' old graveyard, where some forty or fifty others were buried, near a spring on the hill, owned by Dr. Harvey Slaughter. Although I witnessed the interment at nine years old, I could not, nor can any living man, designate his or any other solitary grave, nor are there ten men living that could find the graveyard. This is sufficient to show the impolicy, if not absurdity, of burying in private graveyards.

A SHOOTING AFFRAY

Isaac Bush, son of the original Christopher Bush, of this town, being at Hardinsburg, a dispute arose between Isaac and one Elijah Hardin, son of William Hardin. During the difficulty Hardin shot Bush in the back. Doctors were called in, who proposed to tie Bush while they cut out the bullet. Bush had so much reliance on his pluck that he refused to be tied, laid down on a bench with a musket ball in his mouth, which he chewed to pieces while the surgeons cut, nine inches in length and one inch deep, before they got the bullet, Bush never wincing during the operation.

Hardin being a minor, Bush sued the father, William Hardin, for assault.

The case was submitted to Horace Beardsly, Thomas Owen, John W. Holt, Esq., and Judge James Crutcher, who returned their award at April term, 1804, for $1,500 damages, which was made the judgment of the court. Elijah Hardin was afterward shot and killed by Friend McMahon.

JULY TERM, 1804—A NEW JUDGE

The general court had made an allotment, and on. Henry P. Brodnax was allotted to preside in Henry, Hardin, Muhlenburg and Ohio counties, and took his seat with Haycraft and Munford, assistant judges.

At this time it was the rules of court to spread all bills of exceptions on the order book at length, and to recite the substances of all indictments and presentments, and to record awards of arbitrators and the pleadings. I noticed one exception covering fifteen pages of a large order book.

John Furgeson was the jailer.

OCTOBER TERM, 1804

William P. Duvall, William Watkins and George P. Strauther, Esq., sworn as attorneys-at-law.

Alexander Pope, Esq., county attorney, allowed $80, and the County Court ordered to pay.

APRIL TERM, 1805

Henry Davidge admitted as attorney-at-law.

APRIL, 1806

Joseph Chaffin was jailer, and constable and butcher.

Butchers, by the way, shot down a beef and skinned it on the ground, quartered it as it lay, then taking up smoking hot, cut up with an axe in sizes to suit customers at 1½ cents per pound for forequarter and 2 cents per pound for hindquarter. However, the butcher's first operation was to cut the neck and shanks and shins into small pieces, and a piece of it was put on and weighed with each customer's parcel under the name of mustard.

JULY TERM, 1806—CAUSES FOR NEW TRIAL

In the case of Jonathan Payne against Martin H. Wickliffe the defendant moved for a new trial, and among other grounds alleged that after the jury had retired and before agreeing, did eat, drink, fiddle and dance. And that persons not of the jury were admitted and joined with the jury in drinking, reveling and carousing; and when they were wearied down with their Bacchanalian debauch, concluded to make up a verdict upon the principle of addition and division, each set down his amount, added the whole up and then divided by twelve.

The judge gave a written opinion and descanted largely upon the custom in England—that jurors after they retired were not permitted to eat or drink before they made up their verdict. But as this was a land of plenty, it would not do to apply the rule here so rigidly, as a little necessary food taken in a decent way might strengthen the inner man so as to aid him in his deliberations.

APRIL, 1807

Thomas B. Read and Robert C. Hall admitted as attorneys.

Hon. Thomas B. Read was a tall, portly and handsome man, fond of fine dress, and was a gentleman in his deportment. He removed to Mississippi, from which State he was Senator in Congress in 1826-27, also in 1829, and died suddenly at Lexington, Ky., when on his way to Washington, November 26, 1829. He was in the meridian of life and a man of talent.

CHAPTER XII

OCTOBER TERM, 1807—CIRCUIT COURT

John Moore, Esq., qualified as attorney-at-law.

APRIL 23, 1808

John Miller and James Breckinridge sworn as attorneys.

Jack Thomas admitted as deputy clerk. Jack Thomas deserves some special notice. The county of Grayson was made by the Legislature in the winter of 1809-10. The first term of the court was held in May, 1810. Jack Thomas and Mr. Thornsberry were candidates for the clerkship. Thomas was under 21 years of age, and could not receive a permanent appointment. The Hon. H. P. Brodnax was then presiding judge and voted for Thornsberry. Judge Brodnax decided that a minor could not hold the office, even as a pro tem. clerk, but the two assistant judges decided differently and voted for Thomas as clerk pro tem.

Brodnax decided it illegal and left the bench. and did not sit in that court again until Thomas became of full age, but was always present as a spectator. In that time he became well acquainted with Mr. Thomas and was much pleased with him as an excellent and efficient officer, and ever afterward treated him with great respect, and I cannot give a better history of that excellent man than to republish a letter I wrote to the Louisville Democrat on the occasion of Jack Thomas' death. Here it is:

"ELIZABETHTOWN, July 9, 1865.

"Editors Louisville Democrat:

"I have just learned that my old friend and relation, Jack Thomas, Esq., departed this life at his residence in Leitchfield, Grayson county, Ky., on the 5th day of July, 1865.

"If a man could imagine how he would feel on losing one-half of himself, and yet survive, it might probably approximate my senses of bereavement by this dispensation of Providence.

"Jack Thomas and myself commenced this world poor boys together in the early existence of the State. He was born on the 7th day of February, 1790. His father resided in a house the joiner's work of which was done by Thomas Lincoln, father of the President.

"While Jack was at school (in town) the late Ben Helm, Esq., needed a deputy in 1807 or 1808. He went to the school-room and examined the copy books; the result was that my friend, a ruddy, handsome lad, was chosen as deputy, and a better choice could not have been made in searching the State.

"In October I entered the same office and at once fell in love with Jack, and from that day until the day of his death he and myself were inseparable and devoted friends.

"In May, 1810, he was appointed clerk of the Grayson Circuit Court; also in the same year clerk of the County Court. Soon after (in 1817) I became clerk of the courts in Hardin. We commenced an interchange of services, he assisting me three terms in Hardin and I assisting him three terms in Grayson each year.

"This interchange continued many years, and if I knew any man to the bottom of his soul it was Jack Thomas. He carried his heart in his hand—open, generous, frank. If he knew anything of the arts of duplicity, concealment or deception, I never knew him to avail himself of it. He was a gentleman of the olden time. In due time we each had a family, and each of our houses was the other's welcome home.

"Until he was down by disease he was the personification of innocent hilarity and cheerfulness; his house was the seat of refined and generous hospitality, and nobody could know Jack Thomas as I did without loving and admiring him. He was proverbially an honest, upright man—liberal and charitable to a fault, making all his associates around him easy and happy.

"He was fortunate in the choice of a wife, Miss Jane Hundly, who proved to be in the true sense of the word a helpmate indeed, and for more than fifty years stood by him, the true hearted, painstaking, assiduous and profitable wife and devoted Christian. They litterally lived for their children and united their counsels for promoting the interest, their chief aim being that they might occupy a respectable stand in society. The family consisted of five sons and three daughters, who all surround their father with many grandchildren.

"The season of joy to the united couple was the periodical family gatherings as the sons and daughters stole off from the busy turmoils of life for a season of repose under the paternal roof. Aye, those were seasons of happiness that were felt by others as well as the household and enlivened Leitchfield, and suffice it to say that in the close of life he could look back upon his descendants without the pain of seeing a solitary blot and the most of them pushing forward and making their mark in the world.

"His last illness was painful and protracted, and I regret that I was not permitted to see him from the commencement of the war. But I learn that during his affliction the kind attention of his devoted wife was unremitting. She never left his dying couch for more than a moment, anticipating his wants and administering to his relief as only an angel wife could do. It softened his bed and saved his heart as far as human aid could accomplish—robbed death of its sting.

"May the Lord sustain her under this heavy affliction. But why repine? He has lived his threescore and fifteen years—done much good, set good examples and influenced for good in his circle.

"The first time I visited Leitchfield, some fifty years ago, Jack Thomas lived there; the last time I visited that town Jack Thomas lived there; but now Leitchfield would not be Leitchfield to me—yet why regret? I shall soon follow. SAMUEL HAYCRAFT."

HARDIN CIRCUIT—JUNE TERM, 1808

Present—Stephen Ormsby, circuit judge, and Samuel Haycraft, assistant judge. Philip Quinton, Esq., paid one dollar for contempt. He was a practicing attorney, but I cannot find where he was admitted.

SEPTEMBER TERM, 1808—CIRCUIT COURT

The circuit judge being absent, Samuel Haycraft and William Munford, then assistant judges, held the term; the orders were signed by Samuel Haycraft.

Rev. Benjamin Ogden, a Methodist preacher, was the jailer.

MARCH TERM, 1809

Present—Stephen Ormsby, judge, and Samuel Haycraft, judge.

Samuel Carpenter sworn as attorney-at-law.

Samuel Carpenter resided at Bardstown. Studied law under Judge Brodnax. He was one of the most critical statute lawyers in Kentucky.

He was afterward circuit judge, and was remarkable for the dispatch of business, and the complaint against him was that he met too soon and adjourned too late. Governor Helm, who resided one mile from town, said he was obliged to shave and shirt himself the night before in order to be in court in time in the morning. On one occasion, having business in LaRue court, I stayed all night with my old friend, Daniel Williams, six miles from Hodgenville, when Judge Carpenter was holding court. My old friend gave me breakfast and let me off before day, which enabled me to reach the town before sunup, when I found that the Judge had friend Stone, the clerk, reading the orders before breakfast at his hotel. Stephen complained that he was not allowed to attend to his sick wife, or to eat his meals; but the Judge was inexorable—the business must be done. But at the next term Stephen stretched out the docket so that the Judge was obliged to bring a clean shirt with him, and allowed himself time enough to draw his breath.

Judge Carpenter was also a preacher and made a contribution of $400 to build a Baptist Church in Bardstown, and afterward expended a large amount in completing the house. The church became so largely indebted to him that he became sole owner of the building. Some years afterward he sold the house to the Baptists, for whom it was originally erected.

He left the Baptist Church and connected himself with the Reformers, who styled themselves the Christian Church. He was a rapid speaker and displayed great zeal in the delivery of his discourse. He had an amiable wife and family. He departed this life several years since, and in many respects was a remarkable and conscientious man.

SEPTEMBER TERM, 1809

At the last term Philip Read was sworn in as assistant judge. He was a good judge of law. He removed to Nelson county and lived there a number of years, a prominent and useful citizen.

James Furgeson sworn as attorney-at-law. Furgeson was a lawyer of some note, but was at daggers' points with Judge Ormsby. He kept a note of all the Judge's decisions. Shortly after he quit the practice of law in Hardin and confined himself in Louisville, where he acquired considerable property, but always lived in fear of starving, and that fear pressed upon him so hard that he took his own life to prevent starvation. He died a bachelor. When he started out to practice law he was a fine dressed man and traveled with a servant, in the style of that day, the servant at a respectable distance behind with a large portmanteau on the crupper, a glazed hat in his hand and a brace of horseman's pistols at the pommel—that was the style of the lordly gentleman of that day. But as he grew rich his pride of dress left him and he could often be seen with threadbare apparel.

When Furgeson was sworn in Judge Ormsby left the bench and the court was conducted by the assistant judges—orders signed by Samuel Haycraft.

CHAPTER XIII

HARDIN CIRCUIT COURT—MARCH TERM, 1810

Present—Hon. Stephen Ormsby, and Phillip Read, assistant judge. Hon. James Crutcher sworn as assistant judge in the room of Samuel Haycraft, resigned.

CONTESTED ELECTION

Samuel Haycraft, Esq., last year ran for the Legislature, and was elected over Gen. John Thomas. The latter contested the election on the ground that Haycraft was assistant judge at the time of his election.

The case came up before the House of Representatives and it was referred to a committee, of which the Hon. Henry Clay was chairman.

The committee reported that Thomas was not entitled to the seat, as he was in the minority of votes; also that Haycraft could not hold the seat, as he was in office as assistant judge at the time he was elected, and a new election was ordered. Haycraft having resigned, he and Thomas ran the race over, and by the extraordinary efforts of Thomas' friends he beat Haycraft a few votes.

By an act of the Legislature clerks were required to give a bond in the penalty of $10,000. At this term Major Ben Helm, the clerk, renewed his bond, with Worden Pope and William P. Duval as his securities.

SOCIAL TIMES

At this time taverns were scarce in Elizabethtown. The orators, John Hays and Greenberry A. Gaither, Esq., were regular boarders with Major Ben Helm, the clerk, and to these were added at court times Governor William P. Duval, Worden Pope, Alexander Pope and Frederick W. S. Grayson, Esqs.

I was then a young deputy in the office and ate at the same well-provided table, presided over by Major Helm and his accomplished lady, Mrs. Mary Helm, and at each meal it was a feast of reason and flow of soul as those intellectual and social gentlemen sat around the family board and enlivened each occasion by their conversation and often by their facetious remarks. It opened a new world to me, and I shall ever remember it with a keen sense of delight. But now they are all dead but Mrs. Helm, who is still alive at the age of ninety-two years. She is one of the remarkable women of the time; a kinder heart never throbbed in woman's bosom, always dignified and pleasant, and to this day retains her eyesight so perfectly that she amuses herself in hemstitching without the use of spectacles, living in the same house with her son Henry B. Helm, passing her days in tranquillity, having an independent support, and her delight is to see her friends and converse about religion and about old times, and I have repeatedly remarked that I thought the material of which she is composed is nearly used up.

She was the daughter of the late Benjamin Edwards and a sister of Governor Ninian Edwards, and of Cyrus Edwards and B. F. Edwards, the latter of whom celebrated his golden wedding on the 28th day of September, 1869.

It was my good fortune to be under the tutelage of his excellent lady and her husband, Major Ben Helm, from the age of fourteen until I was twenty-one years old, and to them I owe a debt of gratitude for their wholesome counsel and good example, which I trust has had its influence upon me in a position favorable to my welfare and place in society.

And as my course is nearly run and the sands of life nearly exhausted, being in my 75th year, I hope I will be excused for naming another friend, now no more, for whose kindness to me I can never be sufficiently grateful. I mean the late Hon. John Helm, of whom I have given a sketch in my tenth number. It is a maxim that

A friend in need
Is a friend indeed.

He not only relieved me from heavy pecuniary embarrassments, but gave me his daughter to wife, who has stood by me as a pillar of strength, true and faithful, for more than fifty years.

I omitted to state that at March term, 1810, Frederick W. S. Grayson and Thomas Clark were sworn as attorneys-at-law.

Grayson was formerly and perhaps at that time was clerk of the Bullitt Circuit Court, which office he resigned and removed to Louisville, and there had a lucrative practice as a lawyer.

Thomas Clark was from Virginia; resided at that time in Breckinridge county, and came to his death by eating some poisonous herb which he mistook for Indian physic.

SEPTEMBER TERM, 1810

Hon. Fortunatius Cosby, circuit judge, and Philip Read, assistant judge.

MARCH TERM, 1811

Joseph Allen, Robert Miller and Greenberry A. Gaither, Esqs., sworn as attorneys. Samuel Haycraft, Jr., sworn as deputy clerk. He came into the office in 1809.

OCTOBER TERM, 1811

This term was held by the assistant judges, Hon. James Crutcher and Philip Read. All orders were signed by James Crutcher.

MARCH TERM, 1812

William Little sworn as attorney-at-law. Hon. Judge Fortunatus Cosby presiding.

The Judge was an amiable, pleasant gentleman, was polite to the bar and officers of the court, and had borne a great deal from the bar. About this time rather a rebellious feeling existed among the lawyers, they professing to be able to teach the Judge and openly call in question his decisions. This proved to be the last feather on the camel's back. The ire of the amiable old gentleman was aroused and he determined to put his foot down emphatically and to exact obedience in the bar, and to the dismay of all malcontents, had a rule spread upon the book in these words:

"Be it a rule of this court for the future, that when the court shall deliver an opinion in any case, no member of the bar shall say anything more on the subject, unless leave being first obtained from the court, under the penalty of a fine."

As an obedient deputy clerk, I entered that rule upon the book in my own peculiar copy-plate style.

NOTE—The Judge had just signed a bill of exceptions, and having thus asserted his prerogative, adjourned court until next morning, so that matters might cool down.

Next day, March 12, 1812, Richard Rudd, Esq., sworn as attorney-at-law.

ANOTHER RULE

"Be it a rule of this court for the future that in no case shall more than two lawyers on each side of a case be heard, unless by leave of court."

JUNE TERM, 1812

Horatio Waide produced commission as assistant judge.

SEPTEMBER TERM, 1812

Court held by the two assistant judges, Hons. Squire LaRue and Horatio Weide.

Joshua Novell sworn as attorney-at-law.

Grand jury indicted Barbara Vance for retailing spirituous liquors without license; also for keeping a disorderly house; also for swearing one oath. All true bills.

Barbara kept a doggery in the present Jones house above the Eagle House, the only log house now standing of that ancient date, except the old cabin that the father of President Lincoln lived in. Barbara was rather a heavy case. She had a child one night; next morning she scrubbed her floor and went ahead. She had a suit in court this term against Bill Gibbons for assault and battery. Bill Gibbons was rather a rare fowl—about 6 feet 3 inches high, always ready for fun or fight, whichever was most convenient. He was a saddler, and kept his shop in the same room with Jack Kindle, a tailor. Jack stitched cloth at one end and Bill stitched leather at the other end of the room. Jack was born a cripple, was diminutive in size, but had a large head, full of native wit, and went on crutches.

One day Gibbons was absent and on his return Jack told him that a man had been in who wanted a horse collar, but he did not sell him one. Bill swore that if he refused to sell for him again he would whip him.

Bill was out again and on his return Jack told him that he had sold a collar for him. "Why," says Bill, "it was not finished." "I know that," says Jack; "it lacked a cap, and I gave him a sheepskin to finish it with, and a pair of bridle reins to sew it with."

"Where is the money left Bill?" "Oh," says Jack, "he did not pay for it." "What was his name?" asked Bill. "I don't know," replied Jack. "But I can prove it by a man that stood at the window with a white hat on his head." "And what was his name?" inquired Bill. Jack replied that he did not know.

Bill flew into a rage and was about to slash Jack. But Jack cooled him down by remarking that he was certain of his money, for the purchaser was a Christian. "How do you know that?" says Bill. "Why," says Jack, "I saw him stump his toe and he did not swear."

Notwithstanding Jack was such a cripple, he was fond of a game of cards. One evening Jack, sitting on his counter a la tailor, was pokering with Colonel Miller. Thinking that the Colonel played foul, Jack struck him with his crutch and then hit the Colonel's finger and slid under the counter. The Colonel was asked why he took it. He replied that the little varment seized his finger and ran into an augur hole and he could not get to him.

CHAPTER XIV

A NEW ERA IN THE CIRCUIT COURT SYSTEM—THE ONE-MAN POWER—MARCH TERM, 1806

Present—Hon. Forts. Cosby, sole presiding judge.

Hon. Charles A. Wickliffe produced a commission as commonwealth's attorney.

In charging the grand jury he was pouring a broadside of hot shot into vagrants—that vagabondizing set, sleek and fat; that never worked; snatched a meal here and there; always had money enough to drink and gamble on; a pest to society and an excrescence on the body politic.

An eccentric and honest farmer named Joseph Monin being present in court, was so excited by the speech of the attorney he could hold in no longer and swore that they were thieves and stole their way in the world and ought to be cowhided, tarred and feathered, and at last got into such a frenzy that he pronounced severe anathemas upon men who would not work and continued his loud, vociferations until he exhausted the patience of Judge Cosby, and he ordered Uncle Joe to jail for two hours, thinking that his honest wrath would subside in that time. At the end of the two hours he was returned into court, and it appeared that his pentup wrath had only gained strength and he vociferated louder than ever against vagrants. The Judge sent him to jail for six hours and during that time his indignation abated.

SAMUEL STEVENSON VS. JOHN ECCLES

Suit for the mismanagement as attorney for Stevenson, whereby Stevenson was nonsuited in an action for debt. Judgment went against Eccles, who moved for a new trial. Motion overruled. Eccles appealed. The Court of Appeals awarded a new trial on the ground that the court below instructed the jury that the measure of damages should be to the amount of the debt claimed; that amount had not been established, and therefrom reversed.

The time for suing under the occupying claimant law being about to expire, a tremendous batch of ejectments were brought at this term, which gave the clerk much labor but did him no harm.

The old petition and summons law was then in vogue—a summary way to recover debts.

They were at first set for the third day of the term, but afterward changed to the first day for the convenience of clerks, as it enabled them previous to the sitting of the courts to draw up a lot of blank judgments. The custom of the courts was to inquire of damages in all cases that might come before them. The verdicts were in this form: "We of the jury find for the plaintiff the debt in the petition mentioned and one cent in damages." This plan allowed the clerk for a writ of injury, jury and judgments, and the sheriff for summoning a jury in each case. Perhaps fifty judgments would be rendered in one hour.

This plan continued for years until its working was wisely considered by the Legislature to be needlessly expensive to debtors, and it was enacted that in all undefended cases the jury should be dispensed with and judgment to go by default. This alteration would, under the present clerk's and sheriff's fees, lessen the costs in each case $2.05.

JUNE TERM, 1816

Judge Cosby sat alone during this term and signed the final adjourning order. It was the last of his presiding in this country.

SEPTEMBER TERM, 1816

Hon. Alfred Metcalfe produced his commission from Governor Shelby, appointing him Judge of the Fifth Judicial District, and took his seat.

Judge Metcalfe was an earnest man; was a great favorite of Governor Duval on account of his social and gentlemanly qualities; was a fair lawyer, and the best parlor singer I ever heard. In court he never addressed the officer by name, but it was Mister Clerk, Mister Sheriff and Mister Jailer.

TERM

It was at this term that I had made an arrangement with my predecessor, Major Ben Helm, to resign as clerk, and I was to run the risk of an appointment. Of course it behooved me to do my best for a fair and correct journal of the court's proceedings, as my future prosperity depended on Metcalfe's choice, and I sent my old friend, Worden Pope, Esq., to sound the Judge. He reported to me that he thought that the Judge would appoint me. I replied that that would hardly do. Mr. Pope then said he was fully convinced that the Judge would give the appointment. I still doubted. Mr. Pope then told me that the Judge said he would appoint me. I concluded that would do.

On reading the orders I found I had made more mistakes than I ever had before. But I had relied on the Judge's promise.

Major Helm came into court and very gracefully resigned. I somehow managed to let the Judge know that I was a candidate to fill the vacancy. The Judge asked whom I offered as securities. I had forgotten that requirement, but half the bar volunteered. The bond was given and the Judge swore me. Now, if any one could imagine how a man would feel reprieved from the gallows, he might think how I felt. It was a life and death matter with me, just twenty-one years old, as poor as a church mouse, and a debt of $2,000 to meet, but the result was that by the help of a good friend I got out of debt, and so far have kept out of the poorhouse.

January 20th, 1817, James Guthrie, Esq., sworn as attorney-at-law.

Same day William Farleigh sworn as deputy clerk. He was an efficient and faithful deputy, and although afflicted with a white swelling a great part of the time and which slightly lamed him for life, he never flinched from his duty, and during court times repeatedly wrote the whole night in bringing up the orders of the court. When Meade county was established he received the appointment of clerk, which he held nearly all the balance of his life, thirty or forty years, and there was no better clerk in the State, and according to my opinion, there was no better man.

Shortly after he went to Meade he became a member of the Methodist Church and remained a consistent member until the day of his death. His excellent wife was also a member of the same church. They were counted pillars and their house was always the preacher's home, with the latchstring always out.

March 10, 1817—Benjamin Chapeze, Esq., admitted to the bar.

February 10, 1817—Hon. Alfred Metcalfe, circuit judge, was sworn before the Hon. John Rowan, justice of the peace of Nelson county.

March 12th, 1817—Moses Saltsman, Phillip Saltsman and Lot Dickers put on trial for murder. Not completing the trial that day, the prisoners were remanded to jail and John Haywood, jailer, ordered to summon a guard, not exceeding twenty men. Next day Moses was found guilty of manslaughter and had accommodations assigned him in the penitentiary for two years.

September 1st, 1817—Judge G. A. Gaither appointed county attorney pro tem.

Along about this time the members of the bar became a little pugnacious and many of them were calmed down by adding to the public treasury at the rate of £10 each.

September 5th—William G. Wiggington, attorney-at-law; Larkin Smith, the same. March 9th, 1818, Hon. A. H. Churchill, the same. September 14th, James I. Dozier, the same. September, 1818, was the last term at which Judge Metcalfe presided.

MARCH TERM, 1819

Hon. John P. Oldham came in as circuit judge, and presided until the end of September term, 1820.

JANUARY TERM, 1819

Hon. Paul I. Booker took his seat as circuit judge. He was sworn in on General Jackson's day, 8th January, 1821.

MARCH TERM

Richard Rudd, Esq., produced commission as commonwealth's attorney. June term, 1821—Daniel Poland and Daniel S. Bell sworn as attorneys-at-law. This brings me to the end of order book H.

And with an apology to my readers for boring them so long with the court proceedings, I must take my leave of that branch of the history and go back to the woods again and give a detail of the original buildings and settlers of the town, allude to some early scenes, and afterward I propose to give my recollections of the bar, to be occasionally interspersed with a few anecdotes.

CHAPTER XV

BACK TO THE WOODS AGAIN

As it has been before stated, in the year 1780 the first settlements were made around the present site of Elizabethtown, then Jefferson county, Virginia, and the three forts of Col. Andrew Hynes, Hon. Thomas Helm and Hon. Samuel Haycraft were erected. They were rather stockades, afterward called stations. The manner of erecting these forts was to dig a trench with spades or hoes or such implements as they could command, then set in split timbers, reaching ten or twelve feet above the ground and having fixed around the proposed ground sufficiently large to contain some five, six or eight dwellings with a block house, as a kind of citadel with port holes. That was considered a sufficient defense against Indians armed with rifles or bows and arrows, but with a siege gun of the present day a well directed shot would level a hundred yards of these pristine fortifications. The mode of attack by the Indians when in sufficient force was to try to storm the fort, or by lighted torches thrown upon the roofs of the buildings within to burn out the besieged, but they rarely succeeded in setting fire. If in small force the Indians would shield themselves behind trees and watch a whole day for some unwary pale-face to show himself above the fortification and pick him off. But this was a two-handed game, for it sometimes happened that the red skin in peeping from his tree got his brains blown out. It was very rare that the siege was continued after an Indian was killed, for those Indians were remarkable for carrying off the dead and wounded, even on field of battle. It was a war custom of the Indians never to take an open field fight, but always treed or lay low in the small cane or high grass, and this mode of fighting was more universally adopted by the old and experienced braves than by the young and untaught warriors. If by deploying the whites could get a raking fire upon the red man, they retreated hastily to more distant trees and renewed the fight, and if by force of circumstances they were compelled to come to a hand-to-hand fight they fought with the desperation of demons, using the scalping knife, war axe and war club. The latter was formed of a hickory stick about three feet long and there was fastened to the end a stone curiously wrought from one to three pounds weight, one end of the stone representing the blade of an axe, the other end representing a sledge hammer. A collar was cut in the stone near the end or poll, in which groove the stick was fastened around either by twisting the stick, or with thongs of leather fastening it firmly in the end of the stick, split open so as to receive it. Many of these stone axes are found now in Kentucky. They are always made of brown stone as hard as granite, and when wielded by a strong arm are a formidable weapon. They also used another weapon made of flint, small in size, in the shape of a dart. These were for arrow heads. I have picked up hundreds of them, and nearly every Kentuckian forty years old is familiar with them. The supposition is that this latter weapon was used for killing birds or small game.

In olden times our white boys fastened them to arrows, but not being skilled in archery they were found to be of very little service to them and served only for boyish amusement.

The colony which came to Kentucky with my father, Samuel Haycraft, Sr., consisted of his wife, my mother, Jacob Vanmeter and wife, Jacob Vanmeter, Jr., Isaac and John Vanmeter, Rebecca Vanmeter, Susan Gerrard and her husband, John Gerrard, Rachel Vanmeter, Aisley Vanmeter, Elizabeth Vanmeter and Mary Hinton. All of them, with my mother, were sons, son-in-laws and daughters of Jacob Vanmeter, Sr. Hinton was drowned on the way in the Ohio river. There was also a family of slaves belonging to the elder Vanmeter. These all settled for a time in the Valley.

The most of them opened farms in the neighborhood. The men and women married and propagated at a round rate, averaging about a dozen children, and they have so multiplied that their name is legion and are now scattered over nearly every State and Territory in the Union, and can be found in all grades of society and profession, and of all kinds of names and every shade of color except black—they have not gone into that as yet. There is no vouching for what will be in the next hundred years if the present progressive system of equalization inaugurated by Summer is carried out. But before that happens I hope to be hors de combat, which means defunct.

Other colonists shortly after, perhaps the same year, settled in the Valley. Judge Thomas Helm, with quite a family of children and blacks, came to the same garden of Eden, to-wit, Severn's Valley, and his family, moved by the same impulse, have multiplied and replenished the earth in a very commendable manner. They, too, have scattered far and wide and filled positions of honor and profit equal to any in the State. Then came the Millers, the Thomases, the Browns, Shaws, Fremans, Swanks and hosts of others, who all have done their parts honestly in peopling the earth. They, too, have taken the wings of the morning and (figuratively speaking) flown to the uttermost parts of the earth. These all braved the savages of the forest for years, lived on wild meat, and clad themselves in buckskin and buffalo wool.

These all struggled onward and upward, without any legal organization, but were a law to themselves, and fair dealing and justice was meted out with as liberal a hand as at the present day, notwithstanding the present standing army of governors, judges, lawyers, justices of the peace, clerks, sheriffs, constables, coroners, assessors and tax gatherers. Then no fellow came sneaking in and asked how many acres of land you owned, or how many horses and cows you claimed, or how many dollars you had in the sugar trough under the bed. Nobody was sued for debt, for there was no need of debt, and nobody owed anything but good will; nobody worse false teeth or wigs; nature's food stuck the hair tight, and teeth were not rotted out by using pound cake, syllabubs, sally-lunn, macaroni, chicken salad, stewed oysters or such like conglomerations. A hunter could be on the ground, covered with a buffalo skin and six inches of snow on that, having drunk a half pint of bear's oil, and wake up in the morning cured of the worst cold known in those primeval days.

I have before stated on the first day of June, 1792, Kentucky was made a State of the Union. In 1793 Hardin county was formed. Up to this time the settlers in the Valley had no county seat or place designated for erecting public buildings.

In 1793 Col. Andrew Hynes laid off thirty acres of land adjoining the land of Samuel Haycraft in Severn's Valley, on which to erect the buildings of the county. This place was afterward named Elziabethtown in honor of the lady of Colonel Hynes, whose name was Elizabeth. The difficulties arising upon the question of its being the county seat has been fully recited in the preceding part of this history.

The town was not regularly established until 1797. This thirty acres of land was a rich spot on the side of Valley creek. It was laid off in a singular shape, an oblong square with an obtuse angle at each end, perhaps done so on account of the shape of the Colonel's land, being at one corner of his tract and very heavily timbered with tremendous poplars, wild cherry, walnut, ash, sugar tree, hackberry, hickory, beech, gum, etc., the undergrowth spicewood, dogwood and leatherwood.

After it was laid off into streets and alleys the trustees made several sales of lots at auction. The lots were half acres except at the corners of the public square. These lots were quarter acres. The whole number of lots was fifty-one. The best lots sold for about £3 10s and others went lower. Bidders were slow, as the heavy forests to be cut down and the lots to clear involved in expense three times as great as the value of the lots. But there were found some stout, hearty and strong-armed men patriotic enough to undertake the Herculean task. The first operation was to clear off a spot some thirty feet square in which to erect a round log cabin—puncheon floor and clapboard roof, confined to the house by weight pole, with an eave-bearer, against which the boards rested. As to windows, it is rather doubtful how they were constructed, as there was no glass to be had, and making of a sash was not dreamed of. The chimney was built of wood, with fireplace nearly across the house, never less than seven feet wide in the clear. The first section of the chimney ran up a little higher than the mantlepiece, which was a stick of oak timber about one foot square and about six feet high.

It was walled inside up to that with stone and clay, then the chimney narrowed abruptly to about three feet square, and was constructed with what was then called cat-and-clay, and as some readers may not be posted as to cat-and-clay, I will undertake to enlighten them by a description. First a stiff clay was made, intermixed with straw or grass cut into nibs, then some oak timber was split up into a kind of lath, similar to tobacco sticks; the balance of the chimney was built up of first a layer of clay, then a round of sticks, then clay, and so on until the desired height was obtained, the clay all the time covering the sticks inside and out about three inches thick, the sticks showing the ends about four inches; then a lubber pole was set in across the chimney inside, on which were hung pottrambles, on which to suspend pots and kettles for cooking, boiling soap, rendering lard and heating wash water. The old-fashioned long-handled frying pan was universally used in frying chickens, rabbits and squirrels, turkey breast and venison, etc.

The good dames became very expert in the use of the frying pan. I have often seen them at it when frying pancakes. When one side was sufficiently done the pan was withdrawn from the fire, two or three quick motions were made to loosen the pancake, and then by a sudden twitch up, which nobody except a woman could do, the cake was lifted in the air so as to turn a summersault and was caught in the pan with the done side up and then finished.

The writer has frequently heard discussions among the gentle sex upon the pancake frying art, contending that no woman was a complete adept in the business until she could toss a pancake out at the top of the chimney and run out of the door and catch it in the pan. But understand me, reader, I cannot vouch that this feat was ever performed. It was considered the ne plus ultra of panning.

The length of this number will compel me to defer the inner arrangements of the cabin as to sleeping, loaf baking, turkey roasting, etc., to the next chapter.

CHAPTER XVI

In my last chapter I was building cabins for town houses and went slightly into cooking, and as lightly as some may think of it, that old-fashioned cooking was as far superior to the new-fangled Frenchified mode of macaroni fricassees and gumbo as day is to night, and it would be worth a ride of ten miles on a snowy day to any man of proper taste to partake of a dinner of olden times, but it has been crowded out and can only be found on the outskirts of civilization among the hills. It may possibly have an existence in some of the mountain counties of Kentucky. If so a month spent in that region would restore a man to health and appetite more than double the time at Crab Orchard or Grayson Springs.

SLEEPING

Men, women and children are so constituted as to require sleep, and a comfortable arrangement ought to be made for it. Well, the house is up and covered and the chimney built, then in one corner of the house four forks are let into the ground, shaved poles are placed on either side in the forks and cross-laid with clapboards, then whatever fixing may be on hand, as a bed will be laid on those boards, and laying pride and ambition aside, it is better than the present spring mattresses—that is for the head of the family. Another fixing in another corner is put up for the children.

Next a loft (called in those times upper story) is prepared, and there the boys are put to sleep.

BAKING AND ROASTING

Every family that had pretentions to housekeeping had a bakeoven out of doors, and how was the backoven made, some uninitiated reader will ask. Be patient and hear: First a foundation was made two feet high by setting posts in the ground at each corner; a capping was placed on that, representing sills; on this a floor was laid of split timbers; on this dirt was laid, on that a stiff coat of clay about five inches thick; this was sleeked over by hand or paddle if they had no trowel. Then the oven must go up; a stiff, well-mixed clay was made, intermixed with nibbled straw or grass; then the oven was built of this clay in the shape of a goose egg cut into two parts lengthwise; a square hole for a door was left in front, and a small round hole at the back was made to let out smoke or extra heat. To prevent accidents the builders sometimes laid up carefully dried bark of the required shape for the inside and the oven was built to fit on it. It was then left to dry a day or two. The bark was fired and burn out, which completed the oven and at the same time fitted it for baking. During that operation the oven, first being cleaned of ashes, the door was stopped by a piece of plank and the back hole was stopped up to keep in the heat.

I remember being at an old-fashioned wedding when quite a boy. (Boys went to weddings without being specially invited.) It was at the house of a well-to-do farmer and it was perfectly astonishing to see the quantity of roast turkey, chicken and pig, with huge loaves of bread, puddings, custard and pies, that were drawn out as necessity required. Nothing could equal it, except the rapidity with which it was consumed by the hundred and fifty guests that stood in the house and out in the yard. Perhaps some long-faced cynic may think this history is running into the ground by detailing such minute and trivial matters. I will just say to such that this history is intended to lead the present generation back to first principles and to show off things as they really were in honest home-spun garb. Most historians take up notions full grown and in full blast and leave you to conjecture how they were conceived and brought forth and grew into manhood. Moreover, it was intended to incorporate in this history such inside matter as never was before and in all probability never will again be found in history.

It is absolutely ridiculous for a man not to look beyond his nose. In that view of the case this history is intended for use in future years and perhaps ages. It is intended for the future occupants of Elizabethtown. For who can tell what Elizabethtown will be with her delightful and healthy location, with her enterprising and energetic population, her railroad facilities, her fine water, and her surrounding of intelligent and gentlemanly farmers, the best fruit country in the world, and her future manufactories that must spring up, and when it becomes a large city it will be well to look back upon her starting point.

Excuse this digression. The foregoing description of one house and fixtures and our doings in Elizabethtown will do for all up to the year 1801. The first tanner was Jacob Bruner. The first shoemaker was Joe Donahoe. He kept no shop, but took his kit to the house where a pair of shoes was wanted, or if a whole family were to be shod Joe would do it if kept sober. He sometimes by way of variety was fastened in the stocks, but if a man could keep him sober and bear with tobacco juice he squirted over the floor, he would stick to his last for two weeks at a time in a fruitful family.

The first tailor was a Scotchman named Archibald McDonald. He had no shop or shop board, but tailored around wherever needed. He sat and sewed in a chair like a white man, and by this means was prevented from cabbaging cloth if he had been disposed to do so.

He was also a dancing master, of good physique, wore knee breeches and could outstrut any man in the State. He stood much on his dignity and used high-swelled words. Once in a debating society he was talking of the conglomerations of the superstructure and anatomy of the physical monstrosity called man, and being at a loss for a suitable word, uttered profane language. The president called him to order, and he made the laconic reply "Inevitably" and sat down.

The first mill was built by Samuel Haycraft. It was afterward owned by George Berry and was changed to a sawmill, being frequently put out of order by mischievous youths—like the lamp-breakers of this day.

After this time similar buildings were erected by George Berry, Jacob Bruner, Samuel Patton, Mrs. Jane Ewin, Mrs. Boling, Mrs. Llewellyn, Thomas Lincoln (father of the President), James Crutcher, Asa Coombs, Thomas Davis, Henry Ewin, James Love and David Vance.

Hewed log houses gradually took the place of the round log houses, with shingled roofs fastened with poplar pegs, plank floors and windows with sash and glass or greased paper instead of glass.

The first tavern of hewed logs was built on Main Cross street by James Crutcher and afterward sold to Asa Coombs, who was also justice of the peace.

When Major Crutcher sold that tavern stand he built another tavern house on Main street at the corner of the public square and hoisted a sign of a lion rampant on each side of the board. I remember well I was very shy of that sign and always passed on the opposite side of the street, for stand where you would that savage beast seemed to be staring at you. And from that day (about 1798) to this time (1869) Elizabethtown, to her credit be it spoken, never was without a first-rate eating house and sometimes three or four of them, and that fact has ever made the town a pleasant stopping place.

The first schoolteacher in town that I have a vivid recollection of was a lame gentleman named John Pirtle. He was the father of Judge

Pirtle, now of Louisville. He occupied the Patton house, where Dr. Harvey Slaughter now resides. This house is on the opposite side of the street from the sign of the lion, one square above. This formed another obstacle to my boyish perambulations, as I thought then it was the habit of a school master to slash every boy he could get hold of. So this urchin in passing through this strait of Scylla and Charybdis put on full sail and tacked with considerable dodging, making several acute angles, and always experienced a sense of relief when safely through.

Of Mr. Pirtle, the teacher, I intend in my future number to give a more extended notice.

CHAPTER XVII

From the year 1780 to the year 1800 chimneys were built of wood or stone, for the art of brickmaking had not reached the wooded country. Some of those who emigrated from Virginia might have seen a brick, and if such a material had before that time been seen in this brickless country there is no man living who can testify to the fact. Therefore, I assert without the fear of successful contradiction that no brick was here.

The first stone masonry deserving the name was executed by John Ball on a stone chimney for my father's house. It was a three-story concern, built in the years 1798 and 1799, and took more than one hundred wagonloads to accomplish it. It was fourteen feet wide at the base and was nearly forty feet high. The town by this time was considered to be looking up and had nearly one hundred and fifty inhabitants all told, counting whites and blacks, men, women and children. The public square was nearly cleared off and most of the timber used up, and be it remembered that every half acre had a sufficiency of timber on it to build a house, kitchen, stable and henhouse, and fence the ground, and to furnish firewood for an indefinite time, exclusive of the unwedgeable forked logs rolled together and burned in log heaps.

THE FIRST BRICK HOUSE

About the year 1801 the town was taken completely by surprise by the fact that a brickyard was opened and a brick house was to be built by Major Benjamin Helm, the first citizen that had the means and enterprise to undertake such an improvement. It was a bold start for the beginning. It was fifty feet long and twenty-five feet wide, a deep cellar under the whole building and walled up with huge stone. Two high stories of brick were reared upon this stone wall. The first story was eighteen inches thick and the second story thirteen inches. Charles Sawyer, an Englishman, was the bricklayer, and Robert Huston was the carpenter. One of the lower rooms was wainscoted with panel work of seasoned black walnut presses; two more of those presses were also in the second story. The fire or mantelpieces were massive and curiously wrought of the same kind of walnut lumber. The floors were laid on massive sleepers of blue ash timber. The plastering was done by a Lexington plasterer. The plastering was more than one-inch thick, and the white or putty coat was put on so compactly and well troweled that a man could almost see his face in it. This fine, glossy finish required the expenditure of considerable elbow grease, and up to this time (a period of sixty-six years) there has been no such plastering done in this town since, and the blue ash floors are nearly as perfect as when first laid. I am thus particular in the description of this house, as it was in keeping with the character of the builder, who held the maxim through a long life that "what was worth doing was worth doing well," and to show what difficulties had to be overcome in completing such an undertaking at that early day. There was no lumber yard in the State. The plank was sawed at our water mills or with the whipsaw, and then seasoned by firing in plank kilns. There were no nails to be had short of Lexington.

The Major mounted his horse and rode to Lexington, ninety miles, and rode home on a pair of saddle-bags with thirty pounds of wrought shingle nails—cut nails were not then invented—paying 37½ cents per pound for them. The house was finished in 1803, and as an enduring proof of the fact a circle was made in the street gable about the size of the forewheel of a wagon, made lower than the common surface, finished in white, with these letters:

"Ben Helm.
1802."

The house still stands, having undergone some twenty alterations and additions, and has been owned and resided in by the writer of this motley history from the year 1822—forty-seven years.

The next brick house built was the Court House, in 1805, the brick for which were made and burned on the public square. Of this I have spoken in a previous number.

Next in course of time was a handsome residence built by Major James Crutcher in the west angle of the public square, two stories high, well finished with a set of marble steps in front, being superior in material and finish to anything of the kind in the following sixty years. This house was the hospitable mansion of the Major until about 1818 or 1819, when the Major removed to his palatial residence on the hill, now occupied by J. Robin Jacobs.

The house on the public square was afterward owned by Mr. Hugh Mulholland, an enterprising merchant and clever gentleman, son-in-law of the Major. He added a three-story brick building, filling out to the street. It was sold to George M. Miles, Esq., a most excellent man, who finished the building and lived in it for many years until after the commencement of the late war. During that time Gen. John H. Morgan, of the Confederate Army, attacked the town in December, 1862, with several thousand cavalrymen and about seven pieces of artillery, firing one hundred and seven shots of grape and shell into the town. A ball half buried in the wall still holds its place. Soon after a regiment of Federal troops was stationed in town. One company quartered themselves in an upper room of the house and took possession of the Baptist, Methodist and Presbyterian churches. Mr. Miles being a southern rights man, the soldiers became exceedingly annoying to him, and considering his property and even his life in danger and held by a doubtful tenure, he sold at a great sacrifice to Mr. Andrew Depp, an enterprising German, who has since beautified and much improved it so that it is now the most valuable property in the town.

The next brick building in order was put up by Richard May at the corner of Main Cross and Mulberry streets. This was a most substantial building, but was never finished. Later (in May) he sold it to James Carlisle, who afterward sold it to Benjamin Tobin, Esq., a lawyer, who completed it in good and tasty style, residing in it until his death, which happened in the year 1836. Having no children, he willed it to his wife, Mrs. Martha A. Tobin, who afterward married Sanford J. Poston, Esq. She was a lady of extraordinary attainments and merit, and they continued to reside in the house until the 7th day of August,

1869, when it burned down in the great conflagration which visited our town on that day. Mr. Poston had been an active business man and for many years was a merchant, owned a steam mill, filled the office of sheriff and deputy for nearly twelve years. He tried his luck in California and Texas, and has experienced as many of the vicissitudes of this life in good and bad luck as almost any man living, being frequently cast down but not destroyed. He is a man that says but little and thinks much. If he has sorrows he keeps them to himself; if he is prosperous he makes no flourish about it. He maintains his integrity, is an accommodating, polite gentleman, and according to the rustic phraseology of the day, "keeps a-kicking." He has rebuilt a portion of his residence and is preparing to rebuild the whole. Although he has lived in this town thirty-seven years, few men outside of his confidential friends know him, as it is to them alone he is communicative and with them he is social, while he is civil to all.

The next of note is the Wintersmith House, since called the Summit House. It was intended as the family residence of the late Horatio G. Wintersmith, of whom I intend hereafter to speak, as one of our most valuable and enterprising citizens. The house was on a large scale, with a large brick stable, and was converted into a hotel. After Mr. Wintersmith's death it was sold to Joseph Miller for $12,000. After some years it was repurchased by the heirs, and was finally burned down in the fire of the 7th of August, 1869.

At the same time the three-story brick building at the northwest corner of the public square was built by Hon. John B. Helm, now of Hannibal, Missouri, and was styled the center of attraction. Judge Helm was then and for years before a successful and active merchant and attorney-at-law. This house was substantially built of the very best material and served as a residence, combined with an ample storeroom. It was sold for $6,000 to Brown, Young & Forline. When Gen. John H. Morgan attacked the town in December, 1862, some soldiers were placed in the third-story. A stray ball passed through a window, killed two soldiers and passed through the opposite wall, making a hole nearly as large as a barrel. The house was then owned and occupied by Dr. Samuel Anderson, Sr., an industrious and successful practitioner. He shortly afterward sold it to Mr. Joseph Foerg, a German, who now resides in it with his family, and he is doing a thriving business as a baker and confectioner, and is a quiet and peaceable citizen.

CHAPTER XVIII

OUT OF THE WOODS

About the year 1816 the old houses began gradually to disappear, frame and brick houses gradually and slowly coming in. Tavern houses of wooden structure were on a better scale. Some few years previous to this one was opened on Main Cross street by James Perciful and one opposite by Samuel Stevenson. They had their day. The Perciful House was on the site lately occupied by Bud Hawkins and was previously converted into a brick building and successfully kept by Lloyd Harris, Fielding Friend and Daniel M. Jones, all good landlords, then by Roderick Warfield, a Marylander, a very social, pleasant gentleman, with a fine, intelligent family, such as do credit to any town or city. He afterward sold it to William C. Hawkins, familiarly known as Bud Hawkins. He, with his excellent wife and daughters, conducted a popular hotel and made money for several years. On the 7th day of August, 1869, he was burned out—stock, lock and barrel. Bud always was a thrifty man and made money by honest means in a way that no other man would have thought of. He could snare rabbits, kill more turkeys and deer than all his neighbors put together. This was before he moved to town, and he always made his amusements in that way tell to profit.

One instance will suffice: Mr. B. Frank Slaughter, understanding that Bud's head was level on the rabbit trade, requested him to bring him all he could capture at 10 cents each. The next day, or perhaps the second day, Bud came in loaded down to the guards, and meeting Mr. Slaughter, told him he had brought him some rabbits. "Very well," says Frank, "take them down to my wife and tell her to pay you 10 cents each." When Bud turned off Slaughter asked, "How many have you?" Bud replied, "Only forty!" "Oh, thunder!" says Frank. "Go around town and sell the most of them." After an hour Bud told him that he parted with all but twenty. "Here," says Frank, "is two dollars, but don't bring me another devlish rabbit."

After he opened his hotel, although he was considered a close dealer, he was by no means penurious and never turned a man off because he had no money. He had a good run of custom and highly amused his guests by his wit and comical stories. I have known him to go out and invite half a dozen citizens to dinner, saying, "Come in and take a rough check."

On one occasion a poor man without money, and by no means well, came and stood despondently before his door. Without saying a word Bud saw him and called out, "Come in, sir." The man replied that he had no money. "Ah, well," says Bud, "you are the very man I have been looking for. Come in." He got his supper, lodging and breakfast, and after breakfast he took him to the railroad depot and paid his fare to the next station, where the stranger said he had friends, and on taking leave said, "I will show how I am able to do this," ran his hand into the pocket of his trousers and hauled out a handful of gold and remarked, "If you come across another man in your fix, send him to me."

Hawkins had repaired his back building for his family to winter in, for everything on his lot went with the devouring flames, even his chicken coop, cooking his chickens, feathers and all.

The old tavern stand of Major Crutcher at the sign of the lion was afterward occupied and owned by Daniel Waide, who built a brick addition to the wooden house. He kept an excellent house. His wife was the daughter of Alexander McDougal, a Scotchman and a Baptist preacher of some note, and some people have remarked that all of the preacher's daughters were born scientific cooks. One thing is certain—that no family could excel them in that line. But Waide and his wife both died, and their death was a severe stroke upon our town.

Waide had some of the most accomplished servants in the land. In his will he provided that his servant, Jerry Waide, should be set free on his paying $1,000 to his executor, William S. Young, and in order to enable him to raise the money he was allowed to hire himself at $150 a year. Jerry went to Louisville as a barber, and in less than one year he paid the hire and the $1,000 and soon bought his wife and children and his mother-in-law, and had $500 stock in the Galt House. He was a most courtly and accomplished gentleman in his manners, and before his death accumulated an estate of $30,000.

Since Waide's death the house passed through several hands—Samuel Martin, Esq., and then Denton Geoghegan, and afterward Hugh Mulholland, who removed the wooden structure and put in its place a three-story brick. The hotel was then kept by Mr. Mulholland in fine style. After this Judge LaRue came in. He also married a McDougal, and if any lady could excel their breakfasts, dinners and suppers I have not found them out. Judge LaRue afterward became the owner. After some years he sold it to Thomas B. Munford, who kept up the establishment with equal credit. It finally fell into the ownership of Joseph Tarpley, Esq., and after several changes James E. Talbot became the lessee and now keeps an excellent house, called the Eagle House.

SHOWERS HOUSE

On the old Chalfin stand, at the south corner of the public square and Main street, the old log house has been changed into a large and convenient hotel and is kept by William Showers, more familiarly known as "Big" Showers. He has made extensive improvements in stables, etc., keeps a livery stable, has a strong run of custom, provides good accommodations and a bountiful table. He is aided by an excellent wife as landlady, and well she plays her part.

About the year 1818, John Y. Hill, a tailor, emigrated from Virginia and followed his trade for a few years, but finding stitching too slow a business for a man of his active business habits, he commenced trading in horses. Having built a residence at the corner of Main and Poplar streets and finding the horse trading did not profit, he then commenced burning brick and building houses. He built the Baptist Church, the Hardin County Academy, the house of Mrs. Elizabeth McKinney and the dwelling now occupied by Hon. Judge C. W. Wintersmith. When he quit building it was estimated that he had built about one-fourth of Elizabethtown. He was a popular man and was elected to the Legislature. He was a man of untiring energy, none more so unless we except his wife, to whom he was married shortly after he built his residence. She was Miss Rebecca D. Stone, now universally called Aunt Beck, but with all their energy and untiring industry he became hard pressed. But such a man and woman could not be kept down long. It was admitted on all hands that he was an honest man and all of his old friends were willing to credit him.

When Judge LaRue sold out his hotel, Mr. Hill concluded to make some additions to his house and convert it into a hotel. No sooner said than done, the hotel was opened under favorable auspices. Everything was as neat as a pin, and when a traveler came he was politely met at the door by the landlord in his peculiar, complacent manner, armed and led into a sitting room, and the stranger felt as if he was in a gentleman's parlor. The place had no tavern smell about it, and if ever two little folks were found together who each played their part like clockwork, it was found in John Y. Hill and his wife. They had a fine run of custom, and Aunt Beck's art of coffee making was spread far and wide. But Mr. Hill labored in the vocation too hard. If he had commenced ten years sooner he would have accumulated a comfortable fortune. His valuable life came to a close by over-exertion. He died on the 1st day of August, 1855, and the town felt that a greater calamity could not have happened them. After his death and up to this day Aunt Beck has kept up the house and has proved herself to be a woman of extraordinary administrative ability. She frequently threatened to close her house and quit the business, but she has found that the only thing she does not know how to do and she cannot quit.

Now, if Elizabethtown is not a pleasant place to visit it is not because she has not three first-class hotels. Although in imminent danger from the late fire, fortunately for the town and the community, she escaped that devouring element.

But poor Bud Hawkins' hotel went down, and it is thought that he will rise like a Phœnix and flourish again, to the gratification of his many friends.

CHAPTER XIX

I have in previous numbers spoken of the Baptist Church as having been constituted in the wild wilderness on the 17th of June, 1781, more than eighty-eight years past. The Baptists were the first in order of time in this Valley. Their membership was scattered and covered a great deal of ground. For the accommodation of the church the monthly meetings were held alternately at the Valley and Nolin. These meetings were held in open air or at a private house for many years. Old Nolin Church was constituted in 1803 by a mutual agreement. Up to that time neither church had a regular place to worship. The town church, called Severn's Valley Church, about 1799 or 1800 built a huge log concern on the hill northeast of the Court House. It was of hewed poplar logs. This house was covered but never finished. A rough floor was laid loose and a few break-back benches were set up. The house was used in summer time for public worship, free for all, and occasionally for a school house. About 1805 the house was sold to John Davidson, who removed it to the lot where the clerk's office now stands and put up for a stable. The ground on which the house was first built was sold to Major James Crutcher, on which he erected the fine residence now occupied by I. Robin Jacobs, Esq. About that time my father donated about one acre of ground on the southeast of the town for a Baptist meeting house and a common burying ground, free for all societies.

The Baptist built a frame house on it, which never was finished. About the year 1815 they tore down the frame and erected a large hewed log house with two galleries. This house was finished and held a large congregation. This house was not comfortable in winter and it was customary with the church in the month of October to fix the place of meeting monthly for six months, designating some private residence for each month.

This being the only house of worship, it was occasionally used by other denominations making their appointments at the old log meeting house. About the year 1832 the Methodists, who were now becoming strong, erected the first brick house of worship in the town, in which all the denominations were contributors in some measure. But the largest contributor was Major Ben Helm, who built the house and expended some seven or eight hundred dollars upon it. At that date there was but few better houses in the State.

The Methodists kindly tendered the use of this house to Baptists and Presbyterians and was used accordingly.

Previous to this time the Court House was opened for religious worship and was frequently used by all denominations. So was the old Seminary and many private houses, and particularly the house of Major Ben Helm, under whose hospitable roof the traveling or visiting preachers always found a hearty welcome, and the same hospitalities are used to this day by his son, Henry B. Helm, Esq., who inherits and inhabits the last family residence of his venerable father. Various other places and family residences were open for the same purpose.

The Methodist meeting house some years since was struck by lightning, and in repairing it a considerable addition was made.

About the year 1833 the Baptists and Presbyterians, each considering themselves too weak to build a good house, concluded to build a partnership house, the time to be equally divided. A subscription for that purpose was proposed but did not meet with much favor, and after some weeks' trial was abandoned, only $900 being subscribed. Each house then started separate subscriptions to build separate houses, and in one day's time each had a larger subscription than the united project. The Baptists were fortunate in getting their house built and finished by the late John Y. Hill for $1,200 and he completed it in the second year, this making the fourth house of worship erected by the Baptists. Material and labor then being cheap, the house was finished in good plain style, and such a house could not now be erected under $3,000.

The Presbyterian house was put up and covered in the first year. The funds failing, Mr. Park, a zealous member of that church, finished it the next year at a cost of $500 or more over his subscription, relying on the membership to some day reimburse him. That house has since been much enlarged and improved in every particular, the membership and some friends making liberal subscriptions.

After this the Episcopalians erected a small and neat house of worship.

The Catholics also erected a good house in the west end of town.

These five houses of worship are all standing and regularly supplied up to this time (1870).

CHAPTER XX

The town after 1818 was slowly and steadily built up, so that before the commencement of the war in 1861 from Mulberry street to the public square on both sides there was a solid block of buildings, all of brick. The public square was compactly built all around with brick houses, except two spaces filled by frame houses. After the war commenced until it closed all improvements stopped and if a shingle was nailed on I never knew it. As soon as peace was made a new era began. Nearly all the old roofs were torn off and replaced with new, many old houses were torn down and remodeled, and in two years' time more improvements were made than had been done in twenty years before. In 1842 the town was extended to half a mile square. In the year 1867 the town was again incorporated and its boundary extended to three-fourths of a mile each way from the center of the public square.

This act was repealed and re-enacted with amendments on the 26th day of February, 1868. Previous to this time the spread of the town was retarded by the owners of land adjacent to the old three-acre plot, since which time the land holders east, west and south of the old town boundary have laid out their lands in lots, streets, alleys and avenues, in which additions many lots have been sold at reasonable prices and buildings on these new lots have been rapidly erected.

Splendid residences have been put up by George L. Miles, Rev. Mr. Hagan and Dr. E. Warfield, besides many comfortable and neat residences by other individuals on the west side, and splendid first-class residences on the east side by Col. H. H. Cofer, Capt. W. F. Bell and T. H. Gunter, also about ten other very neat and respectable residences. On the south side, including the old Gallows hill, some twenty or thirty buildings have been put up by the colored population. The African population have exhibited a good deal of energy in erecting their houses of no mean pretentions, and many of them show evidences of thrift.

Two of our citizens, Fritz Raubold and Robert L. Wintersmith, Esq., have showed a good deal of foresight and public spirit in erecting houses in the last named locality for the purpose of renting to such as were not able to build. Additions and handsome alterations and new buildings of elegant finish have been made on Mulberry and Main Cross streets, and up to the 7th of August, 1869, the improvements and additions had at least doubled the previous improvements and extended over five times the area of the original town.

William Wilson, Esq., attorney-at-law, made a purchase of thirty-four acres on the southeast side of the old town and put up a great number of fine outhouses and enclosed the whole in a handsome and elegant style. It is all in the town boundary as extended, an admirable location, and is now decidedly one of the most desirable places in the State of Kentucky for the residence of a private gentleman.

In the last year (1869) many alterations were made on both sides of Main Cross street from Mulberry street to the public square, making the most compact and beautiful part of the town. Those houses were occupied by dry goods merchants, shoe merchants, druggists, saddlers, coffee houses, confectioneries and family groceries, all put up and completed and the rubbish in the streets removed. That street was the pride of the town, giving evidence of enterprise and thrift.

On the 7th day of August, 1869, at about 1 o'clock p. m., some drunken, trifling scamps crept into a haymow of a stable belonging to the Eagle House, which had been kept as a livery stable and situated between the alley and the Baptist Church, and it is supposed they used matches to light their stinking, crooked-necked pipes, and being too far gone in drunkenness to use discretion, communicated the fire to the hay, but drunk as the idle dogs were, they had sense enough to make their escape and the perpetrators are not known to this day. If they had been caught they might possibly have been accommodated with hot lodging. The weather was extremely dry and the flames communicated with great rapidity. Everything on that square on Poplar street, except the Baptist Church and the Seminary, was enveloped in a sheet of flames, and had not the wind favored these two buildings could not have escaped. The fire soon caught to the stable and back buildings on the south side of the alley and from thence to the newly finished fine buildings on the north side of Main Cross street, from which the flames mounted high, and the winds rising, caught across a sixty-foot street into the buildings on the south side of Main Cross street, and in less time than it takes to write this account of it, made an utter sweep of everything from Mulberry street to the public square and on one angle of the square.

The fire raged with such madness and rapidity that a great deal of damage was done in the haste of removing goods and furniture, only a part could be saved, for the fire soon drove everybody out of Main Cross street, and a great quantity of goods and furniture were necessarily abandoned to the devouring elements—all back buildings south of Main Cross street were made a clean sweep of—all the buildings on three squares, and by almost superhuman effort on the part of the citizens, white and black, and even the ladies of the town, the fire was stopped after raging about two hours, and in that short time the hard earning of twenty years lay in ruins.

The loss was variously estimated from one hundred thousand to one hundred and fifty thousand dollars. Several buildings at a distance caught fire, among them was the jail, the Methodist church, Presbyterian church and some private buildings, but they were extinguished without doing much injury.

The great eclipse of the sun occurred just about the time the fire was subdued. The eclipse gave a sombre hue to all nature, well befitting the calamity which had destroyed one-half of the business houses of our town.

CHAPTER XXI

In my last chapter I attempted to give a general description of the great conflagration of the 7th of August, 1869. The town had no engine and no appliances for extinguishing fire except long ladders to ascend upon the roofs, but we have as good a set of fire fighters as any other town. The citizens worked to a great disadvantage, and perhaps the credit of stopping the fire is due in a great measure to Captain J. D. Cole, who at the critical moment took the lead, and by his cool deliberate management had the fire stopped at the southwest corner of the public square, where Wintersmith House connected with the south line of the public square; had it passed that point nothing could have saved the balance of the town.

The losses were about as follows:

1. The large two-story brick of Isaac Radley, fronting on Main street and running back about one hundred feet on the alley, occupied partly in the lower story by Mr. John Ryno as a store room, and back of that as a tinner's shop. Next on the alley was Mr. H. D. Kendall's Coffee House, called the Hole in the Wall. Back of that L. I. Warren's Coffee House, connected with a ten-pin alley running the whole depth of the lots. Loss, $5,000; insurance, $1,600.

2. The three story drug store and residence of J. W. Matthis, Esq., with kitchen and stable back. Loss, $6,000; no insurance.

3. The store house and residence of Jacob Kaufman, a dry goods merchant. Loss, $5,500; insurance, $3,000.

4. The shoe store and dwelling of C. Hotopp. This building had three tenants—one occupied by the owner, the next as a drug store by Dr. Warfield, the next by Joseph Lott as a beer and coffee house. Loss, $8,000; insurance, $1,500.

5. Adam Beeler, as a provision store and sausage factory. Loss, $10,000; insurance, $3,000.

6. John Rihn's shoe and variety store and family residence. Loss, $5,000; insurance, $1,200.

7. The store house of Thomas H. Duncan, Esq., on the corner of Mulberry street, occupied by Duncan & Yeager as dry goods merchants. Loss, $4,000.

Then crossing the street.

8. The large two story residence of Sanford J. Poston, Esq., at the corner of Mulberry and Main Cross streets. Loss, $7,000; no insurance.

9. The confectionery store of Henry Raubold & John Heller building, owned by F. Raubold; family residence above. Loss to the occupants, $4,000.

10. The office attached to Poston's building, occupied by D. H. Gardner, silversmith. Loss, $1,200; no insurance.

11. F. Raubold's residence and bakery, handsomely and newly remodeled. Loss on the two last buildings, $8,000; insurance, $4,800.

12. The store house owned by J. B. Slack. Loss, $2,500.

13. The hotel of W. C. Hawkins. Loss, $12,000; no insurance.

14. The dry goods store house and residence of Antoni Rihn. Loss, $5,500; insurance, $2,740.

15. A. H. Cunningham, dry goods merchant. Loss, $3,000; no insurance.

16. H. G. Wintersmith heirs' Summit House. Loss, $10,000; no insurance.

17. H. M. Middleton, grocer. Loss in goods, $1,600.

18. S. Kaufman & Co. Loss in goods, $3,000.

19. R. L. Wintersmith & Son. Loss in groceries, $700.

20. Duncan & Yeager. Loss in dry goods, $900.

21. Mrs. A. F. Yeager. Loss in fancy goods, $500.

22. John B. Shepherd. Loss of property, $2,000.

23. D. H. Gardner, silversmith. Loss, $500.

24. Mary C. Warfield in drugs and medicines. Loss, $250.

25. G. V. Matthis, druggist. Loss, $2,000; insurance, $2,000.

26. W. H. & L. I. Warren, coffee house keepers. Loss, $800.

The foregoing estimates made by the sufferers.

Besides the losses enumerated—in removing goods and furniture from the buildings not in the burnt district, but threatened to be consumed—much loss was sustained by injury to furniture and beds and covering, and household articles, lost or stolen. Under this head, it is impossible to make an estimate as several valuable libraries were burned, including the valuable law library of the Hon. Charles G. Wintersmith, and the valuable historical library of C. Hotopp, including his German works of rare value, the loss of which he more deeply regretted than the loss of his fine houses. Also the library of Mrs. Martha Poston.

BENEFACTORS

It is due to other towns and cities and individuals to notice their liberality in aiding the sufferers by the fire.

Captain Harry I. Todd, keeper of the penitentiary, sent to Dr. B. R. Young one hundred chairs worth $200.

The citizens of Frankfort, through Thomas Samuels, Esq., assistant secretary of state, contributed $118.

Franklin, through S. Sympson, $12.

Lebanon, through Hon. J. Proctor Knott, $107.50.

The neighborhood of Red Mills, by Wm. Gannaway, in produce, sold for $37.10; cash $2.50.

H. & A. McElroy, of Springfield, $50.

The Louisville and Nashville Railroad Company transported free of charge all the lumber necessary to rebuild and iron fronts free of charge worth more than $2,000.

Through the agency of the Hon. Samuel B. Thomas the last arrangement was made, and a liberal sum in money collected by him in Louisville in addition to his own large donation.

Mr. Thomas also effected an arrangement with the following banks in Louisville: Louisville People's Bank, Bank of Kentucky, Bank of Louisville, Western Financial Corporation, Commercial Bank, Citizens' Bank, Merchants' Bank, Northern Bank, Falls City and Tobacco Bank.

By which arrangement these several banks agreed to loan the sufferers a sufficient sum to rebuild at six per cent, payable in such calls as they could meet. This liberality on the part of the Louisville and Nashville Railroad and the banks in the city of Louisville disproves the old adage that corporations have no souls.

As soon as it was possible for the owners of houses burnt to approach their heated cellars, they commenced clearing off the debris, and in most instances enlarging their plans, and in an incredibly short space of time laid anew their foundations and reared up new and substantial buildings, with iron fronts and tastefully finished a beautiful row on the north side of Main Cross street from the alley at Green row to Mulberry street, with the exception of one on the corner of Mulberry and Main Cross streets all covered with tin.

Among them I would mention the large house on Green row alley owned by Isaac Radley, Esq., with an elegant and spacious store room, finished and occupied in the month of December by our enterprising citizen, John A. Ryno, as a dry goods and variety store. In which store can always be found the pleasant and accomplished clerk, Jo McMurtry, a handsome young man, whose delight is to wait upon the ladies. Back of the store Mr. Ryno has an extensive stove and tin store; this department is presided over by our young friend, Otto Davis, almost as pleasant and likely as Jo, but not quite so blooming.

Back on the same alley you may find H. D. Kendall's Coffee House and R. M. Mock's Gunsmith Shop.

2. The drug store house of J. W. Matthis, Esq., with family residence above, occupied 3rd of January, 1870, by G. V. Matthis and Dr. E. Warfield.

3. The store house of Jacob Kaufman connected with residence occupied in December, 1869.

4. C. Hotopp's Boot and Shoe Store and family residence above occupied in December, 1869.

5. Adam Beeler, one of the most complete provision stores and sausage factories to be found in the land, with a family residence above.

6. John Rihn, boot and shoe and variety store, with residence above.

7. On the south side of the street Mr. S. J. Poston has erected a three story building.

8. F. Raubold has put up a store room and residence above.

9. Antoni Rihn, in addition to his ground, has purchased the site on which Mr. Cunningham's stood, and has erected thereon a beautiful building with two store rooms and family residence above.

10. Wm. C. Hawkins has put up a portion of his building and lives in it.

The energy of all those citizens are in the highest commendable, and bids well for the prosperity of the town, having Phoenix-like arisen from their ashes and donned new and brilliant exteriors, indicative of their determination not to stay put down. They should all not only have the sympathies, but the patronage of a liberal and appreciative community.

CHAPTER XXII

RETRACING STEPS

Having brought the history of building up to the present date (January, 1870), I want to take my readers back and run them up and down on the line of mechanics and artisans who have opened and shut in the town since 1797.

TANNERS

The discovery of the art of tanning leather is doubtless of ancient date, whether it was discovered in the days of Adam I cannot say, for Adam went naked until he partook of the forbidden fruit, then his eyes were opened to his nakedness and he adopted the primitive covering of fig leaves, nor is there any account whether shoes were worn by Noah while he was building the ark. The Bible, which is admitted by all to be the most ancient and reliable history, in the third chapter of Exodus gives an account of Moses beholding a flame of fire in the midst of a bush, and the bush burned not. This exciting the curiosity of Moses, he turned aside to see the sight, and see if he could ascertain why the bush was not burnt. And as Moses approached the place the Lord spoke to him out of the midst of the bush and said, "Draw not nigh hither; put off thy shoes from thy feet, for the place where thou standest is holy ground."

Thus we have it certain that shoes were worn 3,441 years ago, but leaves it doubtful whether these shoes were of tanned leather.

The first account of a tanner by profession is in the forty-first year of the Christian era. His name was Simon, and lived by the sea shore at Joppa, and he must have been a prosperous man, for the Apostle Peter chose his house as a comfortable place at which to lodge and rest himself. But Simon must have learned his trade from some one else, and his boss must have also had a teacher, and so running back to remotest antiquity the origin is unknown. The fact is that tanners are in the world and no historian, dead or alive, has given the origin so we give it up. There are many other things in the world that cannot be accounted for; for instance, how came cats here, and how have they stealthily crept up through all time and made choice of mice for a living. Or who first discovered that oysters were good for human diet? or that tobacco was a decent thing to use in company of ladies particularly, smoking it in crooked necked pipes, and so on ad infinitum.

Moreover there is a kind of posthumous advantage in being a tanner. In Shakspeare's tragedy of Hamlet, Hamlet inquired of a grave digger how long a man would last in the ground? The old grave digger leaning on his spade replied, "If he be not rotten when put in the ground he will last six or seven years, but a tanner will last you full nine years," and that is some encouragement.

The first tanner that I at present remember as operating in our community was one Jacob Bruner, who imagined that the people had worn buckskin moccasins or went barefooted long enough, opened a tan-yard on the ground where the Metropolitan saloon now stands, and commenced operations. Tanners then had no money to buy hides, but tanned on the halves. When a raw hide was brought in the tanner by some mystical operation cut the initials of the owner on the hide about the neck, and entered on a book suited to that purpose the owner's name and the mystic mark intended for initials—and when the hide, if for sole leather, had lain in the lime and bate and tan bark ooze and such decoctions as a tanner only knows—the tail, due-claws and horns taken off and thrown on a shed and the hair in a barrel—in two years or a little less the owner came to draw his share, and then the important point of splitting the hide came off, the tanner always performs it and his knife zigzags in such a manner that the customer never knew which side to take. But the tanner, of course, a disinterested man, advised the customer which side to take—and the owner generally came off second best, but always thought that he had got the tanner badly. This tan-yard went backwards and forwards between the Brunners and the Bruces and the Stouts for several years.

About the year 1805 or 1806 William D. Stone, from Nelson county, bought out the concern and carried on the business successfully up to the time of his death. Mr. Stone also followed butchering beef cattle. The habit then was to kill the beef, the same morning it was cut and sold to customers, by which means his tannery was partly supplied with hides. The profit to the butcher in those days was the hide and tallow. Stone was an industrious and provident man and a respectable citizen, and when he died left an interesting and genteel family—three sons and a daughter. Hayden Stone, one of the sons, resides in Nelson county, and has been the county judge of that county. James E. Stone, another son, is now clerk of Hancock county, and has been for many years, and is a Baptist preacher. He was the father of the lamented Frank Stone, one of the promising young preachers of the state. He was lost by the burning of a steamboat on the Ohio river. His death was a melancholy occurrence. He could not swim, but seeing the only alternative was to burn alive or drown, he knelt down on the boat and devoutly in prayer, committed himself to God, then choosing the flood to fire, he plunged into the stream and for a time seemed to buffet the waves, but finally sank and was drowned. His death was a severe stroke to his pious father and mother, and to his young wife and a numerous host of sympathizing friends.

Another son, Stephen W. D. Stone, Esq., who acted as deputy in my office for several years, and was afterwards clerk of La Rue county and circuit courts, he was and is now an excellent clerk and of high moral integrity. He afterwards removed back to Hardin county, and proved himself to be a fine practical farmer until the late war, when the force of circumstances made it necessary to sell his farm and remove to this town, where he owns a very desirable property.

The daughter married a gentleman named Jonathan McKay, a respectable gentleman of Nelson county. After the death of Wm. D. Stone the yard was purchased by James Park, an excellent worthy man of much promise. But he only lived a few years. After the death of James Park the yard fell into the hands of John Park, a poor, young man of untiring industry. He was cramped for means, but his industry and honest dealings attracted the attention of Hon. John Helm, Sr., who asked Park if he could not get along better with some ready cash. Park replied that he could but that he was too poor to ask anybody to enter as his security. Mr. Helm then said, "I will lend you the money on your own note and your industry will be the security," and thereupon furnished him several hundred dollars. This generous act greatly encouraged Mr. Park, and from that day pushed ahead and eventually established a new yard and in course of time accumulated a handsome estate. He was scrupulously honest and a conscientious man, and a devout member of the Presbyterian church, and was an elder and a pillar of the church, and when he died it was considered a calamity to the community.

Some time after Park commenced, Allen Singleton with Hon. Wm. S. Young started a tannery, which was kept up for several years.

Then Baker & Walker opened a tanyard on the lower end of Main street, which flourished for a while and then went down. Some years since Samuel V. & William Leedom opened a yard near the Presbyterian church. This establishment under the supervision of Samuel V. Leedom, the senior partner, did a fine business up to the untimely death of both partners. Mr. S. V. Leedom was a fine business man, well educated and an accomplished gentleman of unsullied character and an ornament to our town, social and pleasant in his habits and his death was a severe loss.

After the death of the Leedoms the property was sold and the tannery fell into the hands of James B. Slack, Esq., the present holder, and under his management and personal labors he has accumulated an estate of a larger amount than he is willing to acknowledge (as his neighbors think). He seems always to have the cash to buy hides and bark without troubling anybody else. To see him in the streets, with his sleeves rolled above his elbows and his arms dyed yellow with sunshine or tan-ooze, one would not suppose he was worth much. But watch him on Sundays when he goes into the Catholic Church to hear Father Dizney—then he might be taken for a Russian ambassador. Then go to his well-furnished house and see his genteel and accomplished family, and you would conclude that he was a gentleman of the first water. Then go to the board of trustees, of which he had been a member for three years, and you would take him for a man of sense. It was to him we are indebted for the placing of the lights in our streets and for which the trustees got more cursings than dollars when first started, but I think the opposition has abated and the lights have become popular. I do not know that he ever learned the profitable art of hide-splitting, nor do I know that he tans on the shares as in olden times, for I think he buys all his stock of bullock hides, deer skins, sheep skins, hog skins and groundhog skins and sells the manufactured articles to his customers for cash. Now I have said enough about tanners and desist, lest one of them should want to use my hide.

MANUFACTORIES

Elizabethtown is as favorable a location for manufactories as any other place in the State, and it only requires men of enterprise and some capital to make a start. A water course running through the town, abundant water and never failing springs, inexhaustible forests of timber of the best kind, and our railroad and turnpike facilities makes it easy of access.

In the shoe trade we have enough engaged to supply our home demand and much more. First, there is C. Hotopp, a sensible and well-educated German, who carries on the business of shoe and boot making at his new building on an extensive scale, and all who call on him will find him an accomplished and accommodating gentleman, and the only drawback on him is that he is a member of the board of trustees. On matter of policy he will not swerve an inch from what he thinks right, and he generally thinks correctly. Next is our friend John Rihn. Besides his fancy store he carries on his shoe and boot making. He is an honest workman, in proof of which I have in my possession a fancy pair of long-toed, turn-up slippers manufactured in his shop twenty-two years ago, and yet they are in an excellent state of preservation. Next there is William Christen, on Mulberry and Main Cross streets, who has carried on the business successfully for several years. He is a constant worker and an unobtrusive gentleman. Then there is John Heller, who is also a German, with a voice as clear as a bell-clapper, always wideawake. He has some workmen that I cannot say ever go to bed, for as I go home late at night I see them through the window stitching away, and as I return to my office before daybreak I find them still hammering on their lasts. I think John will get along—if he doesn't his journeymen will.

Now I have said enough about shoemaking.

WAGON AND CARRIAGE FACTORY

Dr. H. Baldwin carries on extensively. He keeps a supply of excellent workmen on carriages, buggies, springwagons and road or farm wagons, and turns out most beautiful work, either strong and substantial or light and airy, finished and painted in the most approved style, equal to any in the State. The establishment seems neither to slumber nor sleep, and it would be worth a man's while to spend an hour in going through his establishment. He operates by steam, and makes everything tell. His boiler is in a room where he dries his timber. Then the steam is conducted out to drive his planing mill and sawing machinery, splitting plank from a quarter of an inch to any required thickness, also driving an excellent corn mill. All kinds of blacksmithing is done.

The Doctor is a first-rate mechanic himself, and as a dentist no man in the State can beat him, so far as I know. He has adjoining his factory a neat and handsomely finished and carpeted office, into which he occasionally takes a gentleman or lady, and in short order he fixes up their mouths and teeth to any required shape. He can take a snaggle-toothed man or woman into his shop, take the dimensions of their mouth organs, and in due time turn them out so much improved in looks that their neighbors hardly know them.

Then our friend James B. LaRue and Major Dollins, who established a broom factory a short time since, are running full blast and turning out six dozen brooms daily of the neatest finish, fanciful and useful, and calculate shortly to increase the daily quantity to double the present number. They are Kentuckians, and are making arrangements to supply all the South with the means of keeping clean floors and hearths without going any further north than Elizabethtown. They deserve encouragement, and it is to be hoped they will receive it.

CHAPTER XXIII

It would be impossible for a mortal man to give a detached account of all the merchants who have opened and shut in this town from 1795 up to this date, nor would it add much to this history to do so. Some have come here and set up business and flourished for a brief period of time. Of such it is needless to say anything more than to remark that they came in like a meteor and departed leaving a blue streak behind them, and some were of such light metal that they made no streak at all, except a streak of a board bill on some landlady's day book unpaid. But as a class our merchants have been the most useful and influential men in our community. They labored harder and risked more to minister to the wants and comforts of the people, and to bring to their doors from distant cities not only the necessities of life but extra comforts. All our citizens before the time of merchants wore the home manufactured articles for shirts, coats, vests and pants—so unusual was it to wear store clothes that a boy as a piece of news remarked: "Don't you think Bill Haywood wears a store bought shirt?" How did that come about? Why he dug ginseng, and sold it to Mr. Crutcher, a store-keeper, and he paid him in shirt stuff and some other fixens. Before the merchants bought sugar, tea, and coffee, our worthy progenitors were content to drink sassafras, spice-wood or sage tea, as for coffee there was no substitute, nor was any substitute for the latter article attempted until after coffee was introduced, for after having tasted coffee and a relish for it accomplished, and purses being light in those days, a great many attempts were made to substitute by parching wheat, rye or corn enclosing it in a strong leather apron and with a shoe hammer, beating the mass on the door sill or a flat stone until it was sufficiently pulverized. It was then shook out of the apron into an iron pot, a sufficiency of water poured on it, then adding a sufficiency of maple sugar, (that was not to be grinned at) and some new milk or cream added, and all boiled together, until it was thought to be sufficiently cooked. It was then poured out into a piggen or small pail and placed on the table, which was formed of two long legged stools butted together so as to make the representation of a table, and dipped or poured out into tin cups and eaten with Johnny-cake bread, shortened at that, now don't think that I am going to forget the merchant. I will come back to him as soon as I have told you how a johnny-cake was made. First, every family had a johnny-cake board on hand ready for use. The board was nothing more or less than a thick clapboard about three feet long and six or seven inches wide, shaved smooth with a drawing-knife. Then the corn-meal was worked up into a dough, mixed in with cracklings. Do you know what a crackling is? Well, it is that part of swine's fat that refuses to go into lard. Or if no crackling was to be had, a slight admixture of lard or beef suet was stuck about in it. This mess was skillfully laid on the board, and properly spread, and the board propped up before a good fire. When baked nearly through the skillful use of a case knife liberated the cake from the board, then turned and the other side underwent a baking. Then on the table it went and was greedily devoured and washed down with this coffee. The johnny-cake was first-rate, and as old as I am I would now ride two miles to breakfast with some old lady who understood the mystery. But, alas! for human progress, it has banished the good old johnny-cake and substituted light rolls, corn batter cake and buck-wheat cakes and all such like. But lest you might undervalue the living of our ancestors, they had fried crout, fried bacon, ham and eggs (at five cents a dozen if their own hens did not lay them) sometimes fried chicken, turkey breast, partridge, squirrel or rabbit. But I must stop here for fear I should lose the thread of my discourse in this long parenthesis and return to the merchant again.

It took not only a man of enterprise, but a man of true courage to be a merchant in the days of yore, when there was no stage or railroad, or steam boat. It was a two months' trip to Baltimore or Philadelphia and back. Before starting on this hazardous and laborious trip, the merchant made his will, and called his friends together to take possibly the last leave of them, and it was generally noised over the country before the trip was taken that such a storekeeper was going for goods—I well remembered those times.

The merchant mounted his horse with a brace of horseman's pistols on the cantle of his saddle, led another strong horse with a padded quilt containing about two thousand Spanish dollars—sometimes took a guard through the wilderness part of the way, and thus encumbered traveled about seven hundred miles, this at the best travel would take over hills, mountains and rivers, from sixteen to twenty days—laying in and selecting a stock of goods occupied about three weeks. Then employing several teams of Maryland or Pennsylvania wagons, each drawn by six Conestoga horses, over the mountains to

Pittsburg. That trip occupied from ten to fifteen days. At Pittsburg a flat boat was purchased and the goods stowed away in it. Then the broad horn, as it was sometimes called (in contempt after steamboats started) was floated down the Ohio, the merchant always on board, with his hands and consumed some fifteen or twenty days according to the stage of the water to reach the falls. If piloted over the falls, the boat bound for Elizabethtown and the southern counties would be finally landed at the mouth of Salt River, now West Point. Then the merchant posted off a messenger to his clerk calling for eight or ten wagons to be sent to him. The merchant remaining until the last box, crate, keg or barrel was on the wagons. Then like a bird liberated from his cage, he flew to meet his wife and children. It was a day of rejoicing of which all partook in the neighborhood. And when the wagons arrived the news spread like wild fire that the new goods had come and many a dollar had been hoarded for the occasion.

Now with steamboats and railroads, the same journey is performed in so short a time, that one is hardly missed by his next door neighbor, so brief the absence.

CHAPTER XXIV

Major James Crutcher emigrated from Virginia early in the decade of 1780, and landed at the falls of the Ohio (now Louisville) while the Indians were troublesome. His relations from Nelson and Mercer counties hearing of his arrival, came to the falls to guard the Major and his father and family to Bardstown. The Major hesitated whether to settle in Nelson or Mercer county, but finally stopped in Bardstown and occupied a stone house, which since belonged to Nathaniel Wickliffe, the same house that was afterwards occupied by Melville Vining as a tavern. In this town on the 28th day of August, 1795, his eldest son, Thomas S. Crutcher, was born, the Major having married Miss Gilly Slaughter, and shortly after he removed to Elizabethtown.

He was the first merchant of any note that I remember, in Elizabethtown, he was a resident in July, 1797, for he was one of the first Trustees appointed when the town was established, and remained a citizen until his death. He was then a very sprightly young man, and was remarkable for his neat and genteel appearance and continued so throughout his long life. I cannot say precisely the date he commenced as a merchant but he was in that business at my first recollection of him; my memory extends far back, for I distinctly remember the burial of my grandfather, Jacob Vanmeter, on the 17th or 18th day of November, 1798. But that was an isolated case—the open grave, the coffin and the crowd fastened on my attention so completely that I never forgot it, and it is likely that my recollection more extended does not reach back further than 1800. However, I recollect well some incidents which took place in the old cabin in which I was born, perhaps before 1800; one, for instance, my mother had a pot of hominy on the fire—when she was out I seized a pewter spoon, plunged it into the boiling pot and dipped it out smoking hot, slipped to the door to cool it, when an old gander met me and ran his flat bill into my spoon and gobbled my hominy—and ganders have never been favorites with me since, although the goose trade is now quite brisk in this town.

Judge Crutcher was the main dealer in goods in this town for many years, and was very popular with all the ladies. By some strange perversion of nomenclature he was by half the men and by nearly all the ladies called Crutcher, and it was a daily occurrence to see the good old ladies coming to town to deal in Jimmy Crutcher's store. He has been mentioned several times in the previous part of this history—business of this kind was carried on a small scale for several years, as the sparse population did not justify large importations.

He also dealt in cattle and sent several droves to Baltimore. Now to send cattle to Baltimore by steamboats and railroad would be a light affair in comparison with such an adventure as I am now speaking of. Then there was no steamboats and railroads and very poor roads of any kind; twenty miles a day would be a good drive with a large drove of cattle. The trip to Baltimore under the most favorable circumstances would occupy at least thirty-five days. In returning from one of these trips the Major met with a young man at Martinsburg, Virginia, named Horatio Gates Wintersmith, and prevailed on him to come to the West. Mr. Wintersmith entered the store as a clerk and soon after as partner, and the business was greatly enlarged.

As I intend to speak of H. G. Wintersmith as a merchant and enterprising citizen in a separate article, I will simply continue my narrative of Judge Crutcher. He was the soul of hospitality, and it was his delight to entertain his friends at his hospitable board, and he was generally useful as a Trustee of the Town, Trustee of the Hardin Academy, was Judge of the quarter session court and afterwards assistant Judge of the Hardin circuit court. He represented the county several years in the House of Representatives of the Kentucky Legislature, and was also a Senator of Kentucky and made a narrow escape of being Lieutenant Governor and of a seat in Congress. He was at the battle of New Orleans as aid to General Thomas. His was a useful and active life, laborious and patient in business. His trips East for goods on horse back amounted to an immense travel. One of his trips he took with him a servant man belonging to Major Ben Helm named Charles Slaughter (still living at 93 years). Their route led them across the Youhogeny river, a turbulent, rapid stream, spanned by a bridge thirty feet above the water. The snow was eighteen inches deep on the bridge, which was old and shaky, and in the middle of the bridge two planks were off, leaving a gap two feet wide; the bridge trembled at every step, and then the yawning chasm in the middle but it had to be crossed, it was their only chance; and when accomplished the Judge turned his horse around to look back at his tracks. The Judge remarked, "I was always told to praise the bridge that carried me over safe, but I will never trust that one again." On arriving in Baltimore the servantman, Charles, who always knew which side of his bread was buttered, was not slow in announcing the fact that his master was a Judge.

That was a grand move, and secured to himself as well as the Judge, very marked attention at the hotel. The landlord caught the title and it was "Judge what will you have, shall I send a bottle of wine to your room? Can I make any change to make your quarters more pleasant?" Then the command from the landlord, "Peter, see that the Judge's waiter has a good and early breakfast, for the Judge wants to go out with him in the city."

In short order the merchants were all obsequious. At night the Judge asked Charles how everybody knew he was a Judge. "Why," says Charles, "I had sense enough to tell it." Some years before his death he retired from business and took his ease in the elegant mansion now occupied by I. Robin Jacob, Esq. He was a man of firm constitution until late in life—his health failed and he lost his sight, and died at a good old age, upwards of 80 years.

His son, Thomas S. Crutcher, Esq., is now living, in his 75th year. He is fourteen days younger than myself, a well educated quiet gentleman. We were so near of an age that we might be considered as raised together. We were playmates in childhood—schoolboys together for years, and then he was sent to complete his education under Dr. Hume. He was afterwards a merchant for many years, and lastly, clerk of the Hardin county court. He is a kind-hearted, high toned gentleman.

CHAPTER XXV

TAILORS.

The tailors or artists in cloth, so far as my acquaintance extends, are in the general a clever, neat dressing, gentlemanly class of men; they also have the reputation of being liberal. There is a tradition that nine artists seated on their board, observed a poor man at their door, he was called in, and on investigation he was found to be an object of charity, and each of them gave the poor man a shilling. It was more money than the poor man ever had at one time before, so he determined to try his luck trading on it, and in the course of ten years he found himself rich, built himself a house and on his front door was painted in gilded letters these words: "Nine tailors made a man of me." And hence arose a scandalous perversion of the generous act of the tailors, and the saying is common that it takes nine tailors to make a man, thereby intending to convey the idea that a tailor is but the ninth part of a man, scandalum magnatum.

As I have before stated, Archibald McDonald, a Scottish dancing master, was the first male tailor that ever stuck a stitch in town, and that he kept no shop, but worked around wherever a garment was to be made, and had his board thrown in. Jack Kendall, of whom I have before spoken, was the next I remember. Jack was a dwarfish cripple. One day while Jack was on his board a very slender and rather cadaverous looking man, six feet eight inches high, stopped at the door of

Jack's shop and straightening up to his full height, was taking a view of Jack's dimensions; without speaking a word, Jack in turn was surveying the height of his visitor; Jack spoke first and said: "My good fellow could I get you to pick me a mess of squirrels?"

The stranger replied:

"Certainly you can, and moreover, my name is Jonathan Worrell—I am a crack tailor, and as you are the boss of this shop, and I want to get a chance to help you cabbage cloth."

This struck Jack's fancy and he said:

"If this shop board is wide enough to hold your legs, just twist yourself up here and go ahead. There is a job before you." Worrell understanding all the twistifications of the art, mounted the board and remained with Jack several years. Worrell himself was nearly as droll a genius as Jack.

On one occasion in James Perciful's tavern a wire-walker and a sleight-of-hand conjurer was performing; Worrell came in late after every seat was taken, walking deliberately up to a seated gentleman, making a bow, said: "Sir will you be kind enough to swap seats with me?"

Without thinking, the gentleman arose and Worrell took his seat, and said to Worrell: "Where is your seat, sir?"

"O, anywhere you can find it," and he held on.

The next was Major John Y. Hill, who set up a shop, employed William Greeman and worked together several years, but the Major, of whom I have spoken, was too energetic to confine himself to a shop board and commenced other business, was elected to the Legislature, and finally was a complete hotel keeper and in that business died universally regretted.

Then George W. Strickler carried on for some years, and then retired to a farm and yet lived a respectable gentleman farmer.

About the year 1829 Addison Kinkead with a partner named Wilson, commenced and had a fine custom, but soon dissolved partnership. Wilson left—Kinkead held on and at various times had partners, but the most reliable one was William Showers, better known as Big Showers. Kinkead was a constant worker, a provident man, and accumulated a handsome property—he was always anxious that the customers should have a good fit. The customer would put on the new coat, Kinkead would pull down the tail and slap the man on the back and say, "Big, is not that a bully fit?" then turn the man's face to Big and show him the front and say, "Big, don't you think that fits like a shirt." Big always proved the job well done, and the customer went off convinced that he was fitted to a T, and perhaps he was.

Kinkead afterwards purchased a farm, made a model farmer, and died sometime since leaving a comfortable estate. He was fond of entertaining his friends at his home, and it was done in genteel style and his death was felt to be a loss to our community.

Big soon after quit the board and formed a partnership with Isaac Radley, in merchandising, farming, sheriffing, and even in gold digging in California, and a few years ago opened the Showers House as a hotel, and is yet doing a slashing business, but I think he ought to advertise in the News, as a printer has to live.

Then Warren C. Gray and Cowley set up shops and did well. Cowley has left the State, but Gray still continues the business in this town; is an industrious, good workman and good citizen, and has raised a very genteel family in our midst. Henry Showers and James Moore for some years did a fine business as merchant tailors but in the full tide of prosperity they were burnt out, losing some six thousand dollars of stock. Showers left for the South during the war and was absent about four years—on his return he commenced business for Solomen Kaufman & Co., large merchants. He is very attentive and industrious, and is a quiet, respectable and social gentleman.

Moore after he was burnt out, carried on the business for a while with Jonathan D. McNeil—McNeil married and went to the country for several years. He had served in the army a portion of the time of the late war with credit to himself. He is at present out of business and so is Moore—they were both good artists.

Mr. George Munsch, a German, has also carried on business quite extensively with several journeymen.

CHAPTER XXVI

I had commenced about merchants, but got decoyed off on a side switch, and fell in among the tailors etc., and now take up the merchants again.

The articles of merchandise have varied in different ages.

About the year 1801 Robert Blakely and William Montgomery, two very interesting young Irishmen, came to Elizabethtown and opened a dry goods store with a stock of goods, and soon became very popular. Their store was opened in a log house at the corner of the Public Square, on that spot where the Wintersmith House was afterwards erected and lately burned down. Perhaps their stock of goods was the first that deserved the name of an assortment.

William Montgomery was an Orangeman, and engaged in the rebellion in Ireland in 1798. He was arrested and confined in a prison from which men were taken and executed daily. Montgomery was released from prison through the interposition of his aunt, who was the wife of the Lord Lieutenant of Ireland on the condition that he would emigrate to America.

Shortly after Robert Blakely who was engaged in the same rebellion, evading the officers of the Government, concealed himself in a vessel and thus made his escape to the United States. They married sisters two of the daughters of William Withers, Esq., a very respectable Virginia gentleman near West Point.

About 1820 Montgomery bought a farm near West Point, which was divided between them. Montgomery died about the year 1830, leaving an only son, the late Wm. W. Montgomery, Esq., the father of James Montgomery, Esq., a very prominent young lawyer of this town, and also A. B. Montgomery, Esq., at present a very efficient deputy sheriff.

Blakely remained some years after Montgomery left town, and acted as sheriff for several years, and then settled on the farm and died about the year 1850, leaving a large family of respectable members of the community.

There is something romantic and interesting in the history of these two men. Born on the same Island, engaged in the same rebellion, both compelled to leave to save their lives; emigrating to the same country, finding employment in the same establishment in the city of Baltimore, partners in merchandising in Elizabethtown, marrying sisters, and then living and dying on adjacent farms.

Horatio G. Wintersmith was born at Martinsburg, Virginia, in the year 1786, was the son of Doctor Charles Godfrey Ulias Wintersmith, who was a surgeon in the British army and was taken prisoner by General Gates at the defeat of General Burgoyne. As he was a German and spoke the Hessian language he was put with that corps as a surgeon.

After his capture he joined the American army, and became a part of General Gates' family, and went with him to Philadelphia, where he met with and married a widow Spangler, whose maiden name was Lighter, being the maiden name of his own mother. After which the Doctor settled in Martinsburg, where the subject of the notice was born, and having become much attached to General Gates, his captor, called his son Horatio Gates, which name seems to have been to a great extent in the Wintersmith family.

As has been before remarked, as Major James Crutcher was returning on one of his trips to Baltimore, he came across young Horatio Gates Wintersmith at Martinsburg, and prevailed on him to come to Kentucky—and arrived here in 1806. As I was always intimate with him I have heard him frequently speak on his notions about Kentucky before he came to it. He had been taught to believe they were a semi-savage set of bruisers—wore leather hunting shirts and leather breeches —and they took particular pleasure in knocking a man down if he crooked his finger or refused to drink with him, and that he was astonished on landing in Louisville to see men dressed in broadcloth and acting as polite gentlemen. He entered as clerk in Major Crutcher's store, and shortly after was taken in as a partner.

In about two years after he entered the firm, he was sent to Baltimore to lay in a stock of goods, and as he was a go ahead man, he laid in quite a large stock; so much that the Major was alarmed and expressed some dissatisfaction. Wintersmith had provided for such a contingency, and told the Major that if he entertained doubts about the policy of getting such an abundant stock, that he would take it himself and be personally responsible. And as the Major had great confidence in the foresight and business tact of Wintersmith, with some grains of fear, he acquiesced, and opened a house also at Glasgow, Ky., with Henry Crutcher as a partner, and as proof of his adage, that "ventures make merchants," it turned out that each of the partners laid the foundation of his future fortune upon that importation.

The partnership continued some years when Wintersmith separated from the original firm, and brought many of his relations into business, having married Miss Elizabeth Hodgen, daughter of Robert Hodgen, Esq.

Wintersmith was an energetic business man and of great public spirit, and built largely, and also opened a hotel on an extensive and elegant scale. He was emphatically the life and soul of the town, and was widely known and respected. He was also the cashier of the Union Bank of Elizabethtown which was the only bank of that batch of forty odd independent banks that wound up safe and sound. But in the full tide of life and at the zenith of his prosperity he died January 21st, 1835 in the 49th year of his age. He was married three times, his second wife was Miss Morehead, the third, Miss Jane C. Stovall.

By the first wife was born Charles G. Wintersmith, an eminent lawyer, who served several years in the Legislature of Kentucky, and was afterwards elected Judge of the Court of Common Pleas, which honorable situation he filled with dignity and ability. While a member of the Legislature as chairman of the Committee on Federal Relations he made a report on the jurisdiction of the Ohio river, which was justly esteemed an able State paper.

He also at one time was elected and served as Grand Master of the Grand Lodge of Kentucky and afterwards occupied the honorable position of Grand High Priest of the same order of Ancient York Masons.

Robert L. Wintersmith was another son of the first marriage. I have spoken of him before as a liberal gentleman and enterprising merchant and justly a popular man, but as he has the misfortune to be one of the most laborious Trustees of the town, I cannot answer for his future good name, although the Trustees work like dray horses, they get more curses than thanks.

Major Richard C. Wintersmith was a son of the second marriage. It would be a difficult task to give a faithful pen portraiture of the Major—suffice it to say that he was Treasurer of the State of Kentucky, and during the late war he served with distinction in the Confederate service. He is a portly, fine looking man, possesses a great deal of original wit, a man of decided ability, and universally popular, and if he cannot win a man by argument, he is certain to get him by his humor.

Mrs. Margaret F. Wintersmith, a daughter of the second marriage, a most excellent lady who married her cousin, H. G. Wintersmith, a pleasant and accomplished gentleman, a good merchant and an amateur fruit grower. He was a man of fine taste and a first rate citizen. He left a fine family of children to the care of his widow, and well has she performed the heavy responsibilities which devolved upon her. I have not space to notice any of his decendants except his eldest son, Charles H. Wintersmith, who is a remarkable, sociable, pleasant gentleman, and has made discoveries in the healing art that Esculapius never dreamed of. As he advertises, it will be needless for me to give a list of his remedies. Suffice it to say that they are represented as being sovereign remedies for nearly all the ills, pains and aches that the human family is heir to.

Hon. H. G. Wintersmith is the only survivor of the third marriage. He has been a merchant and Judge of the Hardin County Court and is now a practitioner of law, and raising a fine family. He is a pleasant, polite gentleman, and a zealous member of the Baptist church.

CHAPTER XXVII

Audubon & Rozier were also merchants in town at an early date. Their clerk was James Hackley, who afterwards became an officer in the regular army, one of the most starchy and fine dressing men that ever lived in our town.

This is the same Mr. Audubon who has since been world-renowned as the greatest ornithologist in the world, and has traveled through the United States, Central and South America, torrid, frigid and temperate zones, and has furnished the world the most complete specimens and descriptions of the feathered tribes, from the humming-bird and the sparrow up to the Condor, Ostrich, and Cassowary, with all the grave and splendid plumages that adorn or beautify the birds of creation.

Charles Helm and Samuel Stevenson were once merchants. Helm was a politician and served many years in the Legislature, and in his day the most popular man in the county, and no man could overcome him in an election. He was on Hopkins' campaign, and died several years since; his son, Thomas J. Helm, was for many years clerk of the House of Representatives of the Kentucky Legislature, and was considered the best parliamentarian in the State of Kentucky. He died in Glasgow several years since.

I tried two years under him to master the Latin language, but made a signal failure. Whether it was the fault of the teacher or the scholar I am not able to determine.

After Helm and Stevenson there came up as merchants Major Ben Helm and General Duff Green. They occupied the stand now owned by Judge Eliot—they did business together several years, and as the partners were both distinguished men, special notice of each will be required. Major Ben Helm has been mentioned frequently in the preceding part of this history.

He was born in Virginia on the 8th day of May, 1767, came to Kentucky with his father, Hon. Thomas Helm, and landed at the falls of the Ohio (Louisville) in the fall of 1779, and removed to the Valley in the spring of 1780, then being thirteen years of age, consequently he underwent all the perils of that early day. As soon as courts were established in Hardin county he became prominent in the business of the county, was Deputy Surveyor, and one of the Trustees of Elizabethtown, and made the first survey of the town. He was also one of the first Trustees of the Hardin Academy and held that position for more than forty years. About the year 1800 he was clerk of the Hardin county court, and shortly after received the appointment of clerk of the quarter session court, and when the courts were changed he was appointed clerk of the circuit court, which office he filled up to January, 1817.

Had filled the office of Brigade Inspector for many years.

He was a prudent and provident man, and soon become independent in his circumstances. In the year 1812 there was a call for volunteers under General Hopkins. The Major then being forty-five years of age was a volunteer in Col. Aaron Hart's company, although in affluent circumstances and rather feeble health, he answered to the call of his country. That was a mounted force, each man furnishing his own horse, gun and ammunition, rations for himself and provender for his horse. The force amounted to about two thousand men, there was no commissary or quartermaster, and not a solitary wagon; his brother Charles Helm and George Helm, Thomas S. Crutcher—all of this town in the company; beyond Louisville there was no roads, the route was through the woods, guided by the sun in day and the stars at night. As they progressed they found the Indian towns deserted. When about thirty or forty miles beyond the Tippecanoe, the rear guard of the retreating Indians set fire to the tall grass of the prairie, which burnt with great rapidity, involving the safety of the army, and they would have been destroyed had they not sought a place of safety in a swamp near at hand. Finding it impossible to overtake the wily Indians, and the stock of provisions running low, General Hopkins marched the army back. On the return Major Helm was taken very sick, and for want of an ambulance he had to be carried on a litter between two horses during a march of two days.

The Major was a prosperous and neat farmer, as well as clerk and merchant; he passed a long life of active usefulness, and having a considerable cash capital he was a blessing to the community—was a law abiding man and never exacted any usury, and indulged those indebted to him to almost any number of years. When the Union Bank of Elizabethtown was chartered the Major by universal consent was elected President of that Bank, and his signature to the notes was a passport for their circulation, and as before remarked it was the only bank of the batch of forty independent banks that wound up safe and sound.

The Major was a highly honorable man, temperate in all his habits, and lived to a good old age. He died on the 24th day of February, 1858, in his 91st year. His venerable widow, Mrs. Mary Helm, of whom I have spoken, still lives in this town in her 83rd year.

General Duff Green, the other member of the firm of Helm & Green, was born in Cumberland county, Kentucky, a well educated young gentleman, came to Elizabethtown in the latter part of the year 1812 or nearly 1813 and opened a school and continued some years. It was in this school that Governor Helm was principally educated. He was a man of great energy and a very aspiring man. He volunteered on a campaign against the Indians in the company raised by Gov. Wm. C. Duvall. He styled his company the yellow jackets and on that expedition he proved himself to be a man of undoubted courage.

He received an appointment under the Government to survey public lands in Missouri where he spent considerable time. After marrying a daughter of Hon. Benjamin Edwards, he removed to Washington city, and was there during the Presidency of General Jackson. He was appointed Congressional Printer and took a prominent part in the administration, having become the confidential friend and adviser of the President. Gen. Green was a tall, slender man, with an eye like a hawk, and whatever he undertook was generally accomplished.

It would take a volume to trace Gen. Duff Green throughout his life, his various avocations, sayings and doings. My space will not admit of attempting to follow him, nor am I sufficiently posted, for after he left Kentucky, I never saw him again. But he was a part of the history of our country for more than forty years.

CHAPTER XXVIII

Hon. John B. Helm was born in Washington county, Kentucky, on the 28th day of October, 1797; while in Washington county his father, the late Hon. John Helm, was assistant Judge of the Washington Circuit Court. He lived about eight miles from the seat of justice and at term times he would take little John up behind him on a dashing mare. After reaching Springfield and eating dinner, little John was strapped on the back of the mare, she would take him safely home, being then about seven years old, and his father would remain in court until Saturday night.

Blue grass was then (1804) being introduced into Kentucky. On one of those courts John had gathered a little sack of blue grass seed and carried it behind his father to Springfield where he sold it for a cut half dollar. John thought himself rich and was about the happiest boy in all those parts. A short time after John's mother and several neighbor ladies, who were all great spinners and weavers, concluded to go to Bardstown with their cloth for sale. A separate horse was packed with the cloth and little John was set upon it, like a toad upon a tussock, having his cut half with him, and it was agreed that he should lay it out himself, and was particularly instructed how to address the merchant. After the grown folks had concluded their trading, John's time came, he forgot all his instructions but stepped forward and laid his half dollar on the counter and said: "Sally wants a fan." Sally was his sister, two years younger than himself, and he was much attached to her—and by way of digression I might as well say right here, that this same Sally has been my wife for upwards of fifty-one years, and I hope may be for twenty-five years to come.

A polite clerk said, "Sally shall have a nice fan," and so John bestowed the first money he ever earned upon his sister, in the purchase of a fan about a half a yard long, which opened resembled a peacock's tail. About the year 1809 or 1810 the family removed to Breckinridge county, near Sugartreetown and the Ohio river. When between 8 and 10 years of age he was sent to the Hardin Academy in Elizabethtown, under the tuition of Samuel Stevenson. At this age of the world, the rod was a potent aid to the school teacher and John was whipped to his lessons for about one year, and finally whipped into typhoid fever, which came very near closing his earthly career; when recovered he was taken home and sent to a country school.

Some few years after the Elizabethtown Academy fell into the hands of Duff Green. John was sent to Green's school, and although he was a considerable whipper, he adopted a different course with his pupils—gained his confidence and took great pains in fitting him for an active useful life, and when Green commenced merchandising he selected John as his first clerk in the house of Helm & Green which did a large business. When in this position the author formed a close and intimate friendship with John B. Helm which has continued without interruption up to this time, nearly sixty years. In a few years Green finding that merchandising was too narrow a sphere for his vaulting amibition, went to Washington City, as I have before named.

Major Ben Helm, the senior partner of Helm and Green, purchased the Bush farm. Sally Lincoln, formerly Sally Bush, but now the step-mother of the future President, was entitled to a part of the purchase money—and a portion was to be taken out in the store, and she always brought little Abe to carry her bundles home. Abe would always take his seat upon a nail keg, and John always treated him with a lump of home made sugar, of which barrels were usually on hand in the store. Lincoln never forgot that kindness.

After the store was closed John concluded to study law—went to Frankfort and read law in the office of the Honorable John Pope. After concluding his studies he went to Alabama and went into practice. Afterwards he returned to Elizabethtown and married, and commenced merchandising, and continued in that trade for several years, during which time he built himself a residence, now the property of Rev. Samuel Williams, also built a three story house on the corner of the Public Square, which he called the center of attraction.

There is something remarkable about the Judgeship held by this family. Four generations without a broken link were judges. The great grandfather was a Judge of the Quarter Session Court of Fairfax county, Virginia, his grandfather, Thomas Helm, was a Judge of the Hardin Court of Quarter Sessions, his father was a Judge in Washington Circuit Court, and to wind up he was Judge of the Court of Common Pleas in Hannibal, Missouri.

After settling in Hannibal, Abraham Lincoln then a candidate for the Presidential honors having gone to Kansas on business—and returning through Hannibal learned that Judge Helm lived there, called at his office with his traveling friends, and after making some inquiries in order to identification—as forty years had wrought visible changes in both—Lincoln then turning to his friends remarked: "Gentlemen, here is the first man I ever knew that wore store clothes all the week, and this is the same man who fed me on sugar as I sat upon a nail keg—then minutely related the whole circumstance. Lincoln had a remarkably retentive memory, and never forgot a kindness. After he was elected President, Helm's recommendations were always regarded with favor, notwithstanding they were so bitterly at variance in politics.

My readers will pardon me for taking up a whole chapter with the Hon. John B. Helm—my apology is that I look upon him as one of the remarkable men of the age, and although physically he is a near sighted man, yet mentally he is a far sighted man, and consequently has accumulated a handsome estate. He always was a Democrat in the strict sense of the term and partaken of all my juvenile sports—we differed to some extent in politics, but socially we were a unit.

Alfred M. Brown was a useful citizen of Elizabethtown who began his active life in John B. Helm's store. He was born on Nolynn, a mile from Hodgenville, on Christmas Day, 1811. His father, William Brown, settled there in 1790, on land which had been patented to him by Virginia. One of William Brown's brothers, James Brown, was killed at the battle of Blue Licks in 1782. Another one was Patrick Brown, who was a member of the first Constitutional Convention in Kentucky, but who refused to sign the Constitution because it recognized slavery. Later on he became so convinced of the unwisdom of slavery that he freed his negroes and moved to Illinois where he has numerous descendents now living. William Brown left a large family of children, most of whom have stayed in Kentucky. Among them were John Brown, the merchant of Munfordville, and Mrs. Sarah Churchill, of Mt. Gilead, Larue County.

Alfred Brown came to John B. Helm as a clerk when he was a boy, in 1827. After a few years Mr. Helm made him his partner. He remained his partner until Mr. Helm's death, and was appointed by Mr. Helm executor of his estate. After Mr. Helm's death he continued in the business until 1857 when he was elected County Clerk. He served as County Clerk until the Civil War when, because of his Southern sympathies, the Federal Army in control of Kentucky refused to allow him to be voted for.

During the Civil War he and A. H. Cunningham and Sanford J. Poston were imprisoned much of the time in the Federal Prison at Louisville by the army because of their Southern sympathies. While imprisoned Brown studied law, and after the war was one of the busiest lawyers in Elizabethtown.

He was one of Elizabethtown's most useful citizens. He was one of the first trustees and one of those who contributed largely to the building of the Hardin County Seminary. He was the first School Commissioner of Hardin County, serving without pay, and he laid out the school districts of the county which still stand. He was for several years one of the Commissioners who have held the county's Louisville & Nashville R. R. stock. He made a canvass of the county and published a circular in urging the people not to dispose of their holdings and it was largely the result of his efforts that the county held this stock which in time became of great value.

He married Mary Bell Stone of Bloomfield, Ky., July 10, 1844.

They spent 56 years of married life in Elizabethtown. They had four children—Bell, Edith, Fannie M. and Willie Davis. Fannie and Willie died in early childhood in the dreadful epidemic of scarlet fever that visited the town in March, 1859.

Edith who married Thos. H. Hastings of Louisville died Nov. 7, 1877. Bell who married Dr. Robert B. Pusey alone survived them. Mrs. Brown died Feb. 6, 1900, in her 80th year; Mr. Brown, May 3, 1903, in his 92nd year.

CHAPTER XXIX

Washington Whitaker who was one of the firm of John B. Helm & Co., was born in Bardstown, Nelson county, Kentucky, either in 1799 or 1800. His father, Robert Henry Whitaker, was killed at the raising of his house when Washington was first beginning to crawl. His mother was married to Major Ben Helm on the 17th day of May, 1803, and was immediately located with her son Washington in Elizabethtown, Ky., where he was raised and educated by Major Helm, who treated him as if he were his own son. When grown he commenced merchandising with John B. Helm and Benjamin Helm, constituting the firm of John B. Helm & Co. This firm continued several years and did a thriving business. After the dissolution of that firm in the year 1831, he formed a partnership with Dr. Bryan R. Young but as the Doctor was in full practice in his profession, he could not give personal attention to the business and sold out his interest to Whitaker the same year, 1831. In February, 1832, he took into partnership, Mr. A. H. Cunningham, a young business man who had been clerking for him, and that continued up to Whitaker's death, which occurred 28th of December, 1833.

Mr. Whitaker was an energetic and enterprising man and of untiring industry. His mind was slow in maturing and when he was a boy his mother was fearful that he would make a dull man, but as he grew up to manhood, his intellect kept pace with his body, and when he attained his full height, which was over six feet, with a slender frame, he was a fine looking man, and had a thorough investigating mind, and fine foresight in business matters. He had a fine stock of public spirit and commenced the improvements at Claysville for a tannery on a large scale, which was carried on in his name until his death. He owned quite a number of slaves at the time of his death—he willed them all to Thomas D. and Elisha S. Brown and then they were to be free and sent to Liberia, and the hire fixed upon them was to be divided among the slaves when they departed.

By his will he also provided for his partner, A. H. Cunningham, and by arrangement Mr. Cunningham had the use of $4,000 for five years without interest. He also devised $5,000 to a lady for whom he had a high regard, and the balance of his estate to his step-father, Benjamin Helm, and his wife. His death was a severe blow to the town and was much regretted.

A. H. Cunningham, who has been spoken of in connection with Washington Whitaker, was born in Hardinsburg, Breckinridge county, on the 3rd day of October, 1810—with his father's family he removed to Leitchfield in Grayson county, and on the 28th day of August, 1818, he came to Elizabethtown and commenced as clerk with the house of John B. Helm & Co. When that firm dissolved and Whitaker & Young commenced a partnership, Cunningham went with them and in February, 1832, he became a partner of Whitaker, as is before stated, and continued in that firm until Whitaker's death. Mr. Cunningham was married in May, 1832, to a daughter of the late H. G. Wintersmith. After the death of Whitaker, Cunningham did business alone until the first day of January, 1840—he took in as a partner Lewis Highbough, but he died in 1841. In January, 1848, Major Robert English became a partner for two years. First of January, 1850, Robert D. Geohegan was a partner until September, 1856. At that date J. W. Matthis was a partner and continued to 1st January, 1860. After which Mr. Cunningham carried on the business alone until the 7th day of August, 1869, when he was burnt out. He then sold the ground on which the store house stood and retired from business.

Mr. Cunningham was always a fair trading man and understood his affairs thoroughly, never used any devices or humbuggery to facilitate sales, has his set prices and however anxious he might have been to make a sale—he never pushed an article upon a man, and his was never called the cheap store, but as he was known to be honest and kept correct books—a customer always knew what he was buying—and that it was of the quality represented. And by this straightforward course he has accumulated a handsome estate, and lives well and entertains his friends liberally. I have two reasons for not stating how much of this world's goods he has acquired; first, he is still alive and it would not be prudent to state it, and the second reason is, I am not posted and could not tell if I would.

CHAPTER XXX

Major Robert English, one of Mr. Cunningham's partners, son of Noah English, was born in Virginia, and removed to Hardin county. Robert was a sprightly boy and attracted the attention of the late Horace G. Wintersmith, a merchant before spoken of. Mr. Wintersmith was also postmaster and Robert generally accompanied his mother on coming to town shopping. On one of these visits the postmaster engaged him to carry the mail from Elizabethtown to Leitchfield in Grayson county. In those days a post-rider was looked upon as an important personage, and his passing up and down this thirty miles of road caused as much excitement among the natives as a train of cars would at this time. Persons would collect at certain points to see the post-rider go by, and Bob was not ignorant of the consequence attached to him, and made the most of it. His fidelity and good humor were highly satisfactory to his employer, and he was transferred from the mail business to clerk in the store, and finally a partnership. He afterwards became a partner of A. H. Cunningham, and was in the business several years and in various firms. At length he purchased a fine farm in the neighborhood, and removing to it he soon became a comfortable gentleman farmer. While farming he was elected Sheriff of the county, and then to a seat in the Legislature of Kentucky. He was a kind, liberal and hospitable man, an honest, frank, open-hearted and open-handed man and deservedly popular, and his death was considered a serious loss to the county.

Haden E. English, son of Weeden English, was born in Virginia, on the second day of January, 1815, and came with his father to Kentucky in 1820; in the year 1831 or 1832 he entered the store of Washington Whitaker and continued there eighteen months. In 1834 he commenced as clerk for Hugh Mulholland and continued with him eighteen months, and then married. He then bought the interest of Robert English in the firm of English, Wintersmith & Co., and remained in that firm three years. In 1838 he opened a store in the three story building erected by John B. Helm, and called the place The Center of Attraction, until at last he was called by his intimate acquaintances by the name of Center. He continued in business with various firms up to the year 1848, when he purchased a farm and settled on it and became a prosperous farmer. As a farmer or merchant he was a go ahead man, always polite, a fine talker, and could show up the right or bright side of a piece of goods—a wagon load of corn or oats, fat steer or hogs—and when his crop was growing it was refreshing to hear him talk of it—likes to entertain his friends and knows how to do it—and has the ability to draw upon his dairy for milk and upon his splendid pond for fish, and upon his barnyard for all sorts of feathered fowls—but I must hold in for fear I might overrun him with a hungry company—indeed I know some who domesticated themselves there until their visit became a visitation.

Since I came to sum up the merchants who have done business years back, it would be an interminable job to go into particulars, suffice it to say that there has been more men in this town engaged in mercantile pursuits than any other town in my knowledge of the same limited population.

Bernard Staadeker was born in 1838, Waldorf, Grand Duchy of Baden, in Germany—came to America in 1858—was for some years in the employment of Mr. Schlesinger, and for several years doing business in Louisville. George M. Cresap came from Alleghany county, Maryland, to Kentucky in 1857, and was for sometime in the employ of the Louisville and Nashville railroad. These two compose the firm of B. Staadeker & Co. They have a large stock of goods and are both pleasant gentlemen to do business with.

Solomon Kaufman & Co. Sol Kaufman, Samuel Goldnamer and Joseph Josenberger compose the above firm. Mr. Kaufman came from the city of Mentz, in the Grand Duchy of Hesse Darmstadt, in 1848. Samuel Goldnamer was born in Rhine Bavaria, and came to the United States in 1855. This firm also does a large business on A. Depp's corner—all are accommodating, pleasant gentlemen well educated in their calling. Mr. Kaufman resides in Louisville, the other two live here and have families.

C. W. Yeager & Co., have also opened two stores on Main-Cross street. One of them a fancy store under the special superintendence of Mrs. Yeager, where dress goods, millinery articles, bonnet trimmings, etc., may be had of all shades and varieties. The other store adjoining is the male department.

In speaking of merchants, I omitted to name Charles G. Wintersmith, Sr., a brother of Horace G. Wintersmith, before spoken of. He came to this town several years after his brother, and opened a store of dry goods and was well known and highly respected as an honorable, intelligent and polite gentleman—he was a quiet, good man. He was born in Berkely county, Virginia, September 17th, 1789, and died October 1, 1852. His son Horace G. Wintersmith of whom I have before spoken, was born in Virginia, October 20th, 1811, and died in Elizabethtown, July 11, 1854. C. Godfrey Wintersmith was also a merchant; (first in partnership with his father) and continued for many years after his father's death—he was a perfect gentleman, modest and respectful to all, and everybody loved him. He married the daughter of the late David Cooper Swan, of whom I intend hereafter to speak. C. Godfrey was born 24th December, 1822, and died 26th January, 1859, leaving two beautiful and interesting children, Godfrey and Kate, and as the mother had been dead several years they were left without any parents, but were taken care of for many years by their aunt, Mrs. Mary Crutcher, more familiarly known as Mary Dock, as her deceased husband was a Doctor—and she cared for them with all the tenderness and solicitude that the most affectionate parent could have done.

James West, a splendid workman, who built the house now occupied by I. Robin Jacob. It was built for Major James Crutcher about the year 1820, and although fifty years have passed the work in that house can challenge any work since done in this town for elegance and neatness of finish. West also built the fine house of the late John H. Harlan at Frankfort.

Ambrose Matthis, still living in the neighborhood is a veteran builder, and can show a good deal of fine work in this town.

John S. Cully and Jacob Strickler were also good workmen. Cully was rather a prominent man, very popular, of fine wits, and also served in the Legislature.

I have now gone through a tedious detail of merchants, mechanics, etc.; I may have omitted some but have spoken enough to show that our town has got along in the usual way of slow going towns, as ours has been for many years, but has received an impetus that promises to make it a place of notoriety, and a pleasant place to live and die at. One thing is now, and has been for many years, remarkable for the kindness to the sick and the stranger, a sympathy for the afflicted which does not stop at mere words of condolence, but shows itself in substantial and tangible forms. Many of our citizens have substantial means and some few in affluent circumstances, but there is not found among us that class designated stuck up, or putting on aristocratic airs.

I now propose to go back to about 1785, and speak of the prominent men that figured in those days that tried men's souls—advancing a little higher up, speak of men of note that came in and grew up with the town and have gone the way of all flesh. Then take up the bar and speak of the lawyers who have figured in our courts interspersing it with courts and anecdotes.

Then speaking of the disciples of Esculapius who have figured among us. And conclude with that class who have the training of the young; teachers who have taught the young ideas how to shoot.

CHAPTER XXXI

It is a matter of some delicacy for me to speak of my own father, but as he was one of the very first adventurers to the Valley, as early as 1779, and has been dead for more than 46 years, he has passed into the history of by-gone days, and it would be mock modesty to refrain from speaking of him on account of relationship. His father, James Haycraft, was an English sailor and belonged to the British navy. About the year 1740, the ship in which he sailed touched at some of the harbors of North America, then belonging to the crown of Great Britain, and how he happened to stay, none living can now tell, whether he was discharged or took French leave, none can tell, but certain it is, he liked the looks of the country and concluded to make it his home. He married in Virginia, and had three sons and one daughter; the sons were James, Samuel and Joshua. The mother died, and the father also, when the eldest of the children was 11 years old, and consequently the children learned nothing about their ancestors beyond the vague impressions formed in infancy. They were, as a matter of course, left in a destitute condition. The daughter died while an infant, and James, Samuel and Joshua were taken by Col. John Nevill, a man of wealth, and raised in his house with his son, afterwards General Presley Nevill.

Samuel, the subject of this notice, was born on the 11th day of September, 1752, and at 11 years of age was domiciled at Col. Nevill's where he received a common English education. After becoming of age he left Col. Nevill's, carrying with him a letter of recommendation as a sober, honorable and industrious young man. Col. Nevill, after the close of the Revolution, had an appointment under General Washington as exciseman in the Alleghany country; his business was to assess all the distilleries then in operation. The office was extremely unpopular with the distillers, as it always has been, and always will be; and there sprung up a rebellion called the whisky insurrection. The whisky men came in a body to Col. Nevill's and burned him out root and branch; and the insurrection, close upon the heels of the revolution, had to be put down by an armed force. I have heard my father say that the old Colonel was a man of some education, of great firmness and resolution, rather rough in the exterior, had a noble, kind and generous heart, was in the habit of swearing himself, but woe-be-tide the urchin, white or black, under his control, that happened to utter an oath in his presence. His usual mode of punishment for such an offense was to take off his broad brimmed beaver hat, which he had worn for fifteen years, and had become so saturated with grease as to weigh some ten pounds, and wisping it into a kind of roll, would take the fellow a wallop about the ears that laid him as flat as a pan cake, and saying: "D——n you, do you swear?" But for his sterling worth he was known and esteemed to a wide extent.

Samuel Haycraft entered as a common soldier in the Revolutionary war; served his time out and had an honorable discharge. But while in the army, with his Revolutionary uniform on, as a wedding garment, he married my mother, Margaret VanMeter, in Pittsburgh, Pa., and, soon after leaving the army, in the fall of 1779, emigrated, with the whole VanMeter family, to Kentucky and in 1780 he settled on the hill above the Cave spring, in a fort which he built and in which several families resided. It was in the block house of this fort where my father-in-law, the late Hon. John Helm, was married to my mother-in-law, Sally Brown, on the 22nd day of March, 1787, as has been before noticed in this history.

Mr. Haycraft was identified with and shared in the trials and dangers incident to so early a settlement; in a new country, infested by wild, savage beasts, and the savage Indians, who claimed the country as their own.

It was in this beautiful land of Kentucky that Haycraft, with wife, children and friends, settled down for life; but it was a settlement that had to be fought for in order to maintain it, and if any country in the world was worth fighting for it was this. He participated in all the perils consequent upon the settlement; with the growth of the county he kept pace; served in various offices, as sheriff, judge of the quarter sessions and assistant judge of the circuit court, and represented his county in the Legislature of Kentucky. As he was nearly the first man to build a house in town, and partook largely of hospitality natural to early adventurers and early settlers, he had his full share of custom in court times and elections; men then came forty to fifty miles to vote, and seventy or eighty miles to court, and the most of them got accommodation at the free tavern. When a boy I have known as many as thirty persons lodged and fed of a night, all free. In those days a man would just as soon be caught with a sheep on his back as to charge a wayfaring man for lodging or food, unless he was a regular built tavern keeper.

He was a small farmer; was a good deal in public life; raised a large family and died with a spotless reputation on the 12th day of October, 1823, aged 71 years, 1 month and 4 days.

CHAPTER XXXII

Among the early settlers of this town was Hardin Thomas. He was the father of Jack Thomas, Isaac Thomas, Jesse Thomas, Miles H. Thomas, Alex Thomas, and of several daughters, one of whom married Col. Jacob B. Hayden, our present Senator.

Hardin Thomas was a man of peace. He married Hetty Gerrard, a daughter of really the first Baptist preacher in Kentucky. He was a farmer, and his life was not such as to attract a great deal of attention from the outside world; but he was the "noblest work of God"—"an honest man." And not only an honest man, but was possessed of a degree of benevolence rarely met with in this world of dollars and cents. His house was a kind of central point for the neighborhood; and as at that period, when churches were few, and religious services rather poorly attended to, a little visiting and good eating on the Sabbath day was not looked upon as at this day; on the contrary the folks worked all the week and considered that resting on the Sabbath consisted in visiting friends, having social chats, and a good share of table indulgences. So whether Hardin Thomas and Cousin Hetty preferred it or not, the Sabbath was not a day of rest to them, but rather a day of labor. The neighbors and young folks poured in every Sabbath, or nearly so. I have often been one of them, and partook of the hospitalities of the united head of the family; and those hospitalities were not extended with a stinted or grudging hand, but flowed bountifully from their diligent hands and generous hearts.

And these Sunday doings were not all. But if a penniless man or woman sick, afflicted or distressed, passed through our country, they invariably dropped in to Hardin Thomas' and were there nursed, fed and lodged and kindly treated. And if you have been inclined to insult Hardin Thomas or his wife let one of these unfortunates ask them what was to pay for board, etc.

Everybody loved Hardin Thomas and his wife. He was very popular, but never had any political aspirations or thirst for office. I once heard a man ask Hardin Thomas why he did not offer for the Legislature. His reply was that he "would as soon be found with a sheep on his back." He lived in a house rather better than usual for that day, the carpenter's work of which was executed by Thomas Lincoln, the father of the late President; and the most of that work is to be seen at this day, sound as a trout, although done upwards of sixty years ago.

Hardin Thomas was a man of portly form and a pleasant countenance—just such a one as was comfortable to look at, and was a complete index of the inner man; but many years since he and his good wife have finished their courses and gone to their reward. His mother was a Hardin, the daughter of John Hardin, who was a brother of the old original Mark Hardin, of George's Creek, Pennsylvania. His father was named Owen Thomas; he was the brother of Gen. John Thomas, who commanded the Kentucky troops under Gen. Jackson at the battle of New Orleans. One of his sons, Miles H. Thomas, still lives near Claysville town. He is a clever, honest farmer; and if it was not disparaging to the character of his intellectual powers, I would say that he does not know how to do a mean thing.

One peculiarity more of Hardin Thomas I will name. He was so honest himself that he was unsuspicious of others. And although he lived upon a public road leading from Louisville to Nashville, he trusted all to luck; had no lock to his house, or desk, or smoke-house, or corn-crib. I heard him myself say that there was not a lock about his house. And singular as it may be, I never heard of his losing anything by theft.

But those halcyon days have fled; they have rolled back into the womb of the past, and only held in remembrance by the few aged persons, lingering on the shores of time, who are yet in our midst, but silently and stealthily and steadily approaching the verge of their appointed bounds, and ere long will vacate the seats they occupy, to be filled by younger and stronger men, who in the vigor of youth and manhood shall fill their destiny and in time become old and fade away. But these are rather melancholy reflections, but should not be so, as it is the established order of nature, ever since Adam and Eve were expelled from Paradise; and yet the world is always full of youth, manhood and old age.

The days last spoken of were days of generous hospitality; the size of a man was never taken into account when there was such an abundance of out of doors all around. Apropos Lewis Thomas, who resided on Hardin's creek, in Washington county, was a brother of Hardin Thomas, of whom I have last spoken. He belonged to the Methodist Episcopal Church. In those good old camp-meeting times one was held near his house. On those occasions hundreds, perhaps a thousand, attended who had no camp-building, and were dependent on the hospitality of all the neighborhood around; and Lewis Thomas living on the pebble road, as a living stream of humanity were passing his house, he ran out, and, with a cheerful voice, called on them to stop, adding that his house was only eighteen feet square, but that his heart was one hundred feet square.

The Baptists also had an annual association, which called together immense crowds. On such occasions, at the close of each day's services, there was read in a loud voice from the stand a list of housekeepers who gave invitations to dine, giving their locations and distance from the grounds. It made no difference what kind or size of a house it was, there was always provided an abundance of excellent food and many of the liquors of the day; and as for sleeping, there was no difficulty about that—pallets on the floor down stairs, up stairs, in the kitchen, in the hay-loft, and all around—all were happy and cheerful. I well remember on one occasion of lodging in a room about twenty-five feet long and about fourteen feet wide with upwards of thirty persons. The whole floor was spread with blankets, quilts and mattresses. We laid down in rows, head to the wall and foot to foot, and all slept well. On such occasions the negroes caught the spell of their masters, and would hail passers-by to stop, saying: "stay with us, we have more people here and more to eat, and better cooks than they have over yonder. So round to and come in."

Once upon a time there was an association held with the Mill Creek Baptist Church in Nelson county, about three miles northeast of Bardstown. The venerable Benjamin Edwards and his most excellent wife were members of that church. His place was called Shilo. He was the father of the late Gov. Edwards Dr. B. F. Edwards, Cyrus Edwards and Mrs. Mary Helm, of our town, still living. On that occasion he gave a general invitation, and 100 came to his house and were fed and lodged for three days in a most comfortable manner. A little episode occurred on the Sabbath morning before starting to church. The 100 mouths exclusive of the thirty in the family ate up more fresh meat than had been provided. The old gentleman was quite a stickler for the observance of the Sabbath, but here was a difficulty, and asked the counsel of Gardener Grundy, one of his guests, and Brother Grundy soon settled the point by saying, "Rise, Peter, slay and eat." Accordingly, up went for the hogs, and all were provided for.

Speaking of the negroes who were their servants, they felt identified in interests with their masters, and were true to defend their character or property, and if be, to fight for them. Old General Braddock, a negro man and slave of one of my uncles, took his rifle and went a campaign against the Indians, and he says he killed nine of them, for which he was awarded his freedom.

Although a little out of my boundary I will relate a matter that was told to me by the late Rev. Marcus Lindsay, a Methodist preacher. A settlement of several families at Harrod's Station, near Harrodsburg, cultivated jointly a field a little distant from the houses. Some one of the settlement owned a little runt of a negro, and he was reserved as common stock to help the women. The men went to the field in the morning, stationing one of the party as a sentinel. His duty was to watch for the Indians and give the alarm, but it so happened that a party of Indians had, before being noticed, gotten between the farmers and the house and were rapidly pushing forward. The alarm was given, but not soon enough to prevent a powerful Indian force entering a house before the door was closed. The little negro, immediately yoked in with the Indians with all the vim of a Billy-goat. The Indians soon floored the little negro, and while attempting to stab the negro the woman of the house seized an axe and at one blow split open the Indian's head and killed him. The little negro crawled from under the Indian, shook himself and said: "Now, Mistress, let in another," supposing he could go through the same feat. And it was merely accidental that the negro escaped. The Indian having that morning killed a woman who had on an apron, this he took from her person and tied it on himself, covering his knife, and in fumbling about the apron for his knife he lost his life.

This incident is related to show the feelings between master and servant in those days.

CHAPTER XXXIII

Ambrose Geoghegan, Sr., was born in the city of Dublin, in Ireland, on the 30th day of March, 1753, and graduated in Dublin as an engineer, and was in other respects an accomplished scholar.

This family is noticed in Macaulay's History of England as being one of the party that espoused the cause of King James, the Second, who was deposed, and William, Prince of Orange, in conjunction with Mary, his wife, ascended the throne; and when king William invaded Ireland the Geoghegans were found in arms. Ambrose Geoghegan while yet a single man emigrated to America and landed in Baltimore on the 6th day of May, 1771, and was married to Peggy

Zelman on the 6th day of May, 1777; and after losing his wife, married again in 1784. He was living at Hagerstown, in Maryland, until about 1804, when, with his sons Denton, Thomas and J. H. Geoghegan, came to Kentucky and stopped at the Crab Orchard, in Lincoln county, and while there purchased of Armstead Churchill the Hynes Station track, part of which is now in Elizabethtown. The deed bears date of 1805, and recognizes him as a citizen of Lincoln county. His grandson A. D. Geoghegan, Esq., says he arrived at Hynes' Station on the 21st of February, 1808. But that must be a mistake as the deed bears date of December 29, 1806, and recognizes him as a citizen of Hardin county. Immediately after coming to Hardin the family purchased several adjoining farms.

Ambrose Geoghegan, Esq., was an old man when he came to Kentucky, and was possessed of considerable means, was an accomplished engineer and surveyor, and, moreover was an accomplished gentleman and of social disposition, and soon formed the acquaintance of the principal citizens of the town and neighborhood, and, in order to cultivate friendly and social relations, got up a Whig club, which frequently met, when the free interchange of ideas and discussions on the subjects of the day were well calculated to make friendship and brighten up society.

The first celebration of the 4th of July was a barbecue dinner with a speech and toasts that I ever remember of was gotten up by him, and was freely participated in by all the gentry of the county; and by his example and under his influence the state and tone of society was greatly improved. His son, Thomas, died soon after he came to Hardin county, leaving an only daughter, who at an early age married John B. Wathen; and they are both dead.

The oldest son, Denton Geoghegan, Esq., was a large farmer for several years, and finally settled in Elizabethtown, where he resided until his death, on the 5th day of April, 1850.

He was for many years a justice of the peace; was a remarkably clear-headed man, strictly honorable in all his dealings, and noted for his punctuality. He raised two sons and several daughters. One only son survives Ambrose D. Geoghegan, Esq.; he is also a large farmer, stands high in this community, and has all the traits constituting the clever gentleman—social, generous, hospitable and kind. One daughter, Rebecca, married Col. Chas. Cecil, who wisely gave his sons a thorough education, and they have proved themselves to be energetic, thorough-going men, and they have succeeded in establishing one of the most popular colleges in Kentucky, known as Cecilian College, about six or seven miles from Elizabethtown and about a quarter of a mile from the Elizabethtown and Paducah railroad, the stopping place for which, is Cecilia Station. The College is presided over by Henry A. Cecil as President, and Thomas G. and A. D. Cecil as Professors; and a more accomplished and gentlemanly trio would be difficult to find.

John H. Geoghegan, the last and youngest son of A. D. Geoghegan, Sr., inherited the old homestead, Hynes' Station, and lived there until he died, on the 11th day of January, 1854, aged 75 years. He was a correct, upright citizen of regular habits. He was rather peculiar in his habits and manner of life; wrote a beautiful hand, and took note of all passing events that he deemed worthy of remembering; was fond of a gun; kept a good one, and by the way of recreation, made havoc of small game, but was too systematic to let it interfere with his business, which was that of farming and he was a model farmer. He reared a considerable family—six sons and two daughters. The sons were Dr. Thomas D. Geoghegan, Dr. Ambrose E., Dr. Denton, Robert D., John H., and William S. Geoghegan. His house and his hand were open to his relations and friends. He raised his sons to work, and in their younger days worked side by side with his colored servants. He was a kind master and provided bountifully for their wants, and allowed them great privileges. He gave his sons as good an education as the country afforded. Three sons studied physics, and became excellent doctors of medicine. The oldest, Dr. Thomas D. Geoghegan, settled at West Point, Hardin county, and had a successful practice during his life. The Doctor's location favored an extensive practice, living at a point where Hardin, Jefferson and Bullitt counties connect, and in four miles of Meade, on the Ohio river, the lines between Kentucky and Indiana. His practice extended largely over all the above-named counties, and in two counties in Indiana. This heavy practice, of course, kept the Doctor much from home. On one occasion a man came for the Doctor, and while waiting employed himself in reading the sign on the shop, "Dr. Thos. D.

Geoghegan." The name is pronounced Go-ha-gan; and the man in waiting not being an apt scholar, made it read Dr. Thomas gone again. Becoming tired, he left for some two hours. On returning and looking at the sign, he exclaimed, "There now, I'll swear he's gone again."

He died suddenly on the 9th day of December, 1863, in the fifty-second year of his age, leaving a very respectable and intelligent family.

Dr. Ambrose E. Geoghegan, after studying his profession, married in Leitchfield, and opened practice there for several years, then returned to Elizabethtown, and had a successful practice for several years, and during that time discovered a powerful medicine, composed of prickly ash, smart weed, walnut leaves, brandy and sugar, so concocted as to produce a pleasant medicine called "Hydropiper"—no doubt a very valuable discovery, and its merits not yet fully tested. In partnership with Dr. Young and Slaughter, a large quantity was manufactured—still not sufficient to meet the demands, for its fame spread far and near.

The Doctor now lives at River View, in Jefferson county—a very pleasant, social gentleman, and one of the finest talkers in creation.

Doctor Denton Geoghegan, was born at Hynes Station, April 23, 1824; remained with his father and labored on the farm until 1842. He then went to Mississippi and followed the brick-mason trade for two years, and returned home with greatly improved health and began the study of medicine under his brother, Dr. Thos. D. Geoghegan, at West Point, and graduated at the Medical College in Louisville in 1846; then practiced at West Point until 1854; then removed to Elizabethtown and practiced there until his death, which happened Nov. 16, 1869.

He became a member of the Episcopal Church, and was a liberal practitioner, never charging widows or preachers; was a kind master, and had many excellent traits of character, but never married. His death was unexpected and much regretted.

Robert D. Geoghegan, our enterprising and accomplished merchant, has been spoken of in a former part of this history. He is a valuable citizen, and a useful member of the Methodist Episcopal Church.

Jno. H. Geoghegan, Jr., is a farmer, and lives in Nelson county. The youngest son, William S. Geoghegan, was also born at Hynes Station, and resided with his father until his death, and then with his excellent mother until her death, in the year 1860. Soon after this he became an assistant in the store of his brother, Robert D. Geoghegan. Billy is a good worker; has a fine flow of spirits; and as to his age I need not say, as he is a single man, and, from all appearances, is likely to remain so.

CHAPTER XXXIV

Jacob Vanmeter, Sr., was my grandfather. He, with his family, emigrated from Monongahala (called by the old folks "Monongahale,") in 1779, landing at the falls of the Ohio that fall, and in the year 1780 came to Severn Valley and settled on the farm now owned by George W. Strickler, two miles from Elizabethtown, on Valley Creek, at the mouth of Billy's Creek, on which last-named creek he built a grist mill for corn and wheat; and although there remains at this day not a vestige of that mill, yet I ought to know where it stood, as my father carried on a one-horse distillery, and when I was about eight years old it was my daily business (Sunday excepted) to go with a bag of corn three times a day. My grandfather continued to reside there until his death, which occurred on the 16th day of November, 1798. He was in the original constitution of Severn's Valley Baptist Church on the 17th day of June, 1781. His wife (my grandmother), his son, Jacob, and his negro man, Bambo, were also members.

At his death he left a large family, all grown. It is now nearly seventy-two years since his death, and, like the old patriot Jacob, his descendants have multiplied like a fruitful vine that ran over the wall, for they are scattered East, West, North and South, and may be found in every State and territory in the Union, and from the least calculation that can be made they now amount to at least 3,000 souls. And that will not appear so surprising when you are informed that one out of his numerous grandsons had his thirtieth child born the night of his death. But that was over the average of the family, as the number of the most of his descendants to each family ran on an average from nine to eleven children, but frequently exceeded those numbers. My mother had eleven.

My grandfather was buried on his own farm, I was present at his interment, being then three years and three months old, and have a distinct recollection of the occasion. His son Jacob procured a sand rock and cut a tombstone, which is yet in good state of preservation, and every letter distinct at this day. On the 5th day of February, 1849, I visited the grave, having a little grandson with me, and pointed out to him (as one of the fifth generation) the spot that contained the remains of his great, great grandfather. And as the inscription itself on the stone is a piece of antiquity, particularly as to its orthography, I will here give something like a facsimile of it:

"HERE LIZES
THE BODY OF
JACOB VANMATER
DIED IN THE 76
YARE OF HIS AGE
NOVEMBER THE 16
1798"

The spelling is rather of the normal style, and is an honest attempt to carry out the sound. Thus the word year is spelt YARE, containing all the proper letters of the word, but misplaced; but the sound as spelt in the epitaph is precisely as he always pronounced it for nearly ninety years. Therefore, let no man pretend to criticise it or alter it. It is a jewel to me; so all mankind let it alone. It is the honest home-spun epitaph of a good man and Christian who braved all the perils and dangers of his day honorable, kind, hospitable and generous, and truly a patriarch.

Jacob Vanmeter, the second, was born in Berkley county, Virginia, October 4, 1762; became a member of the Baptist Church at eleven years of age. At nineteen years of age, say 1779-80, he came with his father to Kentucky and settled in the valley.

And here I will remark that I am not writing for a religious paper, but it is impossible to write anything about Jacob Vanmeter the second without touching upon religion, I must be indulged, for although his life was one of industry, toil and thrift, yet it was all the time a life of religion.

At the death of his father he inherited the old homestead. On the advent of the Geoghegan family he sold them his farm and settled at the folks of Otter Creek, where he built a large stone house and resided in it until late in life. When all his children had married and left him he then sold out, and with his wife, resided with his son John until he died. He was rather an extraordinary man, of true patriarchal stamp. He was always regarded as a firm pillar of the church, and during seventy-eight years of his membership he was never under church censure or discipline. He departed this life on the 12th day of December, 1850, in his eighty-ninth year, having been a member seventy-eight years, and forty-five of the time a Deacon, leaving thirteen children, the youngest upward of forty years of age. Out of his ten sons seven were Deacons in the Baptist Church. Three days before his death he led at the family altar of his son John. His prayer was uttered with great fervency and was protracted beyond the usual length. At the close he had to be assisted from his knees. The family offered to put him to bed, but he would not permit, saying that he wanted to speak of the goodness of God; and he sat in his chair he repeated hymn after hymn from Watts. The family remarked that they had never heard him repeat them before. He said that the Lord had strengthened his memory and brought to his mind hymns that he had learned sixty years before. Like Moses on Mount Pisgah, sight was strengthened to view the promised land. He had often prayed to be released from the pangs of death. A few minutes before his death he exclaimed, "the light! the light!" His daughter-in-law, who was at his bed side, supposing that the light of the window disturbed him, offered to close the blinds. "O, no," said he, waving his hand, "the glory of God filled the house; he has kept me under the hollow of his hand from a child." Then adjusting himself for burial, closed his mouth and eyes, crossing his arms, with his right hand upon his heart, without a struggle or a groan, and evidently without a pang, like a shock full ripe, was gathered to his father. Thus lived and thus died the last survivor of the old pioneers of the Church at Elizabethtown, a godly man and a shining light.

Abraham W. Vanmeter, son of the last-named, Jacob, was born in Hardin county, two miles from Elizabethtown, April 1, 1789. He resided in Hardin county up to the year 1831, when he removed to Tazwell county, Illinois, where, in 1866, he lost his faithful wife, who for sixty years had been a Christian helpmate in the true sense of the word. Shortly after the death of his wife he sold out and took up residence with his son, Edward A. Vanmeter, a merchant at Burlington, Iowa, and resided there in great peace and tranquility until his death, on the 11th day of November, 1868, in the eightieth year of his age. He embraced religion at an early age, and was a true pattern of Christian piety, and aided much in building up the church wherever he lived. He was the father-in-law of the Rev. Doctor Weston, an eminent preacher of the City of New York, and was the father of the Rev. Wm. C. Vanmeter, now of the same city, who is known nearly world-wide for his labors in the Five Points in that city, and then in the Howard Mission, in another ward. He has been the most laborious and untiring man in gathering up little cast-off wanderers, snatching them from degradation and vice, and to the number of many hundreds procured genteel homes in the West, and mostly in Christian families; others were taken care of in the city, clothed, fed and educated.

W. V. Vanmeter, in furthering his plans of benevolence, has visited London and Paris and many cities in Europe. But the scene of his arduous labors has been in the city of New York. A full account of his labors and the stirring scenes through which he passed would make a volume of thrilling interest.

It would require a volume to give a history of all the Vanmeters, but the object of this history will not allow it. They constitute a tribe or nation to themselves, and this number must suffice for that family, and I hope that my friend and relation, Doctor Samuel Vanmeter, of Charleston, Indiana, will not take exception to my not saying how he rose to fame and wealth in his profession; he can take care of himself.

CHAPTER XXXV

Among the remarkable men, who at an early date were citizens of Elizabethtown, might be named the late John Morris, Esq. He came to Elizabethtown about the year 1812, when about twenty-three years of age, then an active, stout man. He was an Irishman by birth, and was an excellent hatter, and commenced as a journeyman of the late Hon. Horace Waide, who was also a hatter, and at that period, was an assistant Judge of the Hardin Circuit Court. At the death of Judge Waide, Morris commenced a shop on his own account. He was an industrious honest man, and prided himself on being able to make a hat that would last a careful man four or five years.

In those days Sunday hats were not worn every day, and some hats of that description would be kept on hand in tolerable credit for ten years. The fashions did not change so often as they do now-days; they were the bell-crown style, very high, and contained as much material as is now used in three, and a man could put in the crown two dozen apples, and a half dozen eggs and walk ahead without suspicion of a cargo aloft. This fashion was found convenient to boys who visited orchards or hens' nests. Morris was a generous, social man, but the Irish blood which predominated in his veins, made him a quick, high-tempered man, and in his youthful days he frequently broke over bounds. He was raised in a Presbyterian family in Cincinnati, and although wicked, was taught to hold in high reverence preachers of the gospel, and to pay due respect to religious services. As a striking instance of his habits, by some means a coolness existed between him and the Rev. George L. Rogers, a Methodist preacher, so that they were not on speaking terms. His shop was diagonally across the street from Rogers, who was also a wheelwright and turner. While Morris was working a hat in the kettle, preparatory to blocking, some man at the time was in front of the preacher's door, abusing and cursing him in a violent manner. This attracting Morris' attention he stepped to the door and in a very decided manner informed the man, that if he had his hat out of the kettle he would thrash him for cursing the preacher. The man replied that he would wait on him and see who could whip. Morris, in a short time, got his hat out, and stepped into the street with his sleeves already rolled up; they engaged in a fight and Morris chastised him by terrible blows and dexterous kicking, until the fellow was completely subdued, and then told to go his way and mind how he cursed a preacher again.

A few years after this Morris married a Miss Mollie Larue, by whom he raised a family of children; and they lived together in great comfort. One of his sons, William L. Morris, studied and practiced law, but afterwards was an able Baptist preacher. Morris being a man of high integrity was appointed a Justice of the Peace, and then Sheriff of the county, and finally elected County Judge. He proved to be a man of fine business habits, and was called upon to act as guardian, administrator and executor of more estates than any other man in the county, all of which he closed to a cent. When he took up an opinion upon any subject, it was next thing to an impossibility to move him from it, and the argument of lawyers before him had very little weight. On the trial of some case before him, he had listened with impatience and disgust at the speaking of three lawyers. Young Owen Thomas, the attorney who had the conclusion, arose to speak, when the Judge said, "See here, Owen, you may speak if you like, but I tell you my mind is made up." He said his aim was always for justice and the law ought always to bend to justice.

On one occasion, a man was tried before him for stealing a colt—a witness for the defendant was evidently swearing to downright falsehoods, until the Judge losing all patience said, "See here, my good fellow, you are swearing to a pack of lies—stop right there, and begin on a new platform and tell the truth, or I will leave this bench and give you a thrashing." And thereupon, the fellow being alarmed, commenced again and told an entirely different tale, with something like the semblance of truth. "Now," says the Judge, "that looks a little more like the truth, but you are such a liar, that I have not full faith in your story yet, and I will guess at the matter myself."

On another occasion, a party in the country was out on a coon and opossum hunt, and got on a general drunk, and late in the night laid down in the woods and slept until day. On awaking at daylight, one of the party saw his coffee pot in the ring and asked how it got there, One of the party, a negro man, answered that he had brought the whisky out in it. The owner of the coffee pot went to Squire Morris, and took out a warrant against the negro for stealing his coffee pot. The whole party were arrayed before the Squire, and he patiently listened to all their tales, after which he arose from his seat and remarked that from their own showing they were all a low, dirty pack of good-for-nothing fellows, and now every one of you forthwith leave my office, or I will kick every one of you out, which was in due time accordingly done.

In 1832, Squire Morris joined the Baptist church, and after this he deserved great credit for the command over his temper; made a useful member up to his death—he was the most earnest man in his profession—knew no guile, but was truly a matter of fact man, as well in the church as in public life—he was liberal in his contributions and his house was the preacher's home. He married the second time—his last wife was of the Edwards family—was the widow of Isaac

Adair, and the first and last wife, added much to his domestic comforts, and they always met his friends in a pleasant hospitable manner. His second wife also died before him. He was born on the 27th day of March, 1789, and died on the 6th day of March, 1865, and his death was a serious loss to the town and church.

Rev. John Pirtle was born in Berkley county, Virginia, on the 14th day of November, 1772; was married to Amelia Fitzpatrick, a native of Hampshire county. He determined at once to come to Kentucky. Here I will take the liberty of quoting a paragraph from Redford's History of Methodism in Kentucky.

"In those days it was the habit of persons who intended coming to this country to rendezvous for more than fifty miles around, at some place appointed, and travel in company with arms in their hands. Mr. Pirtle and his wife, both young and recently married, had come to one of these points of meeting, and found they had mistaken the day—that the company had gone two days before. But as they had determined to come to Kentucky, and had received the blessing of their friends at the home they had wept for at parting, they resolved that they would not go back, they would come to Kentucky, and accordingly he with his rifle on his shoulder, on one horse with a pack under him, and his wife on another horse with a pack under her, traversed the solitary wilderness, and crossed the mountains alone; not on the old wilderness road, but on the old wilderness path, till they came to Crab Orchard. Then every rustle of the leaves or crack of a stick in the deep woods, might well have been taken for the whereabouts of the prowling savage.

He settled in Washington county, Kentucky, and in the year 1799 removed to Elizabethtown, where he taught a school a short time, and acted as deputy clerk for Major Ben. Helm.

I was then quite young, and had an idea that it was the duty of every school master to slash every boy he met, and as I have previously remarked, always passed in double quick on the other side of the street.

Mr. Pirtle removed back to Washington county in 1802. In the year 1809 he connected himself with the Methodist Episcopal church, and became a powerful preacher. He was a man of natural eloquence, and of impressive personal appearance. And the celebrated Barnabas

McHenry said that he had the best voice he ever heard, and the late Rev. Marcus Lindsay, who was himself an able divine, in preaching his funeral after his (Pirtle's) death in 1826, said he was of the clearest intellect and strongest mind he had ever known.

He was a man of expansive and vigorous mind—well trained and methodical. He had remarkable talents in mathematics and especially delighted in astronomy, and so profound was his knowledge of that abstruse science, that he could make his calculations in it as easily and rapidly (says his son, Judge Pirtle), as he could in arithmetic.

After settling in Washington county the second time, says Mr. Redford, he raised a large family of children, all of whom except one became members of the Methodist church.

CHAPTER XXXVI

In my last number I spoke considerably at length of that remarkable man, John Pirtle. When he removed to this town, his son, the Hon. Henry Pirtle, was a small babe, and as he was once an infant citizen of our town, I take the liberty of saying a few words about him. He was born in Washington county, Kentucky, on the 5th day of November, 1798, and was carried in his mother's arms to Elizabethtown in 1799. When he approached manhood he studied law under the Hon. John Rowan, at Federal Hill, Bardstown, Ky., commenced the practice of law at Hartford, Ohio county, and soon after removed to Louisville. After becoming established, he was appointed Judge of the Circuit Court and General Court, and held that office from October, 1826, to January 2, 1832, when he resigned. Again, 1846, he was appointed Circuit Judge, but held the office only one term, and resigned. Gov. Crittenden then appointed him Chancellor of the Louisville Chancery Court in March, 1850. He was then elected under the new Constitution, and held the place until 1856, was re-elected in 1862, and held this office until 1868. All the time he was Judge or Chancellor he devoted to the practice of law. He was a State Senator from 1840 to 1843, being the only political office he ever held.

In 1846 the law department of the University of Louisville was organized, and he was made Professor. He still occupies the chair, and lectures twice a week to two classes, and in that situation he takes great pleasure.

After this history it will be needless to say that Judge Pirtle is a profound lawyer and able jurist, and through a course of many years, has deservedly held the high esteem and confidence of the community, well befitting the descendant of the Rev. John Pirtle, whose advent into Kentucky with his heroic young wife entitled them to a niche in the temple of fame second only to the immortal Daniel Boone.

And as the old house in which he resided in Elizabethtown has become classic, I must be indulged in giving a short history of it and its occupants. The lot containing one half an acre was originally purchased of the trustees on the 10th day of September, 1798, at the Statutory price of an oath, five shillings. Rawlings hastily put up a hewed log house, about twenty feet square, without a chimney, the timber of which, or most of it, being cut down upon the lot. That was done in 1798-99. In 1799 John Pirtle rented it and moved into it, and lived in it until 1802. After passing through several hands, on the 8th day of March, 1804, it fell into the hands of Samuel Patton, who married a daughter of Major Wells, of Revolutionary fame. Patton lived in it until 1806, during which time he put up a brick chimney, and on the back of the chimney inscribed these letters: "S. P. 1806," and that chimney to this day fixes the locality of the alley running by it.

In 1806 Patton sold it to John Davidson, from Virginia. He resided in it until 1809, and during that time weatherboarded the house and hid the "S. P. 1806"; so that it did not see the light of day for sixty-four years, and then only looked out for one day, and was shut up again. In 1809 John Davidson sold it to his brother Thomas, who only lived in it one year; and in 1810 he sold it to John Eccles, Esq., who was originally a shoe and boot maker, but was then a lawyer of some note.

Eccles resided in it until the 19th day of February, 1814, when he sold it to Gen. Duff Green, who resided in it until 1817. He has since become known world-wide.

In 1817 Gen. Green sold the premises to Elias Rector, of Missouri. Rector never lived in it, but sold the property to the late Hon. Benjamin Chapeze, a distinguished lawyer. He resided in the house until the 14th of April, 1828, when he sold it to Thomas J. Walker, a soldier, who resided in it until shortly before his death. The house has had numerous tenants in it of short periods. One of them was Montgomery Mason, a hatter. On the 17th day of June, 1835, the present occupant, Dr. Harvey Slaughter, purchased the property of Wathen's executors, and resided in it ever since. The Doctor at various periods, made several additions and alterations but it still had an antiquated appearance, by no means suited to the Doctor's taste, he being an eminent physician, a literary man, and fond of the poets; but still his house was on a par with those of most of his neighbors, and he philosophically submitted to its rural appearance, with the majestic locusts before the house, which embosomed the building and lent something of majesty and the grandeur of the feudal times of old England and sometimes pallisading or entrenching himself behind the poet who sang:

"I knew by the smoke that so gracefully curled
Above the green elms, that a cottage was near;
And I said, if there's peace to be found in the world,
The heart that is humble, might hope for it here."

So it stood for thirty-five years. But it so turned out, in the course of human events, that in August, 1869, a great portion of the town was burned down; and upon the ruins sprang up, like a Phoenix, new and tasty houses, and many houses, such as Dr. Warfield's, Dr. Short's, Hewitt's, Prof. Heagan's, Judge Cofer's, Capt. Bell's and Commissioner Gunter's, in addition to the fine business houses in the popular part of the town.

The Doctor looked out upon this, it became the last feather on the camel's back, and he determined to stand it no longer, and called in the aid of Architect Turner, and off came the old weather-boarding. And such a remodeling and demolishing of the old place, and such a metamorphosing has not been witnessed in the town for seventy-eight years. The tall windows, weighted sashes, magnificent doors, splendid Venetian blinds, chaste and heavy cornices—the whole matter rearranged, renovated and renewed—walls painted a dazzling white, window blinds a heavy drab, sash cherry color, with French glass; nothing gaudy about it, but presents a sober, chaste and classic appearance.

The Doctor still retains and protects the venerable trees before his domicile with all the sacred care that the ancient Druids did their grand old oaks in their mountain fastnesses.

Thomas W. Nicholson, a schoolmaster, came to Elizabethtown about the year 1805. He wrote a splendid hand, was a tolerable English scholar, a strict disciplinarian, and understood the use of the birch to perfection. He was rather a dandy for that day, and wore a fine blue cloth coat and ruffled shirt, and buckskin pants of elaborate finish. These pants he regularly covered with yellow ochre on every Saturday, and usually spent half the day drying them, and he considered them the height of gentility. He preserved strict order in his school; and as it was the custom in those days for boys to walk several miles to school, they brought their dinner in baskets, which were all put on a bench, and each boy or girl stood in front of his or her basket. Thomas Kennedy, being the largest, stood at the head, and repeated with solemn face, these words: "Sanctify, we beseech Thee, O Lord, these creatures to our use, and ourselves to Thy service, for Christ's sake. Amen."

Nicholson brought with him a fine black horse. At the end of nine months a report reached the town that the horse had not been fairly obtained. This report coming to Nicholson's ears, he departed one night with his horse, leaving a trunk of clothing and his tuition fees uncollected, and has never been heard of since, now 65 years.

Samuel Stevenson was about the next in order of succession of teachers in Elizabethtown. He came about the year 1806, and, on the old system, was a good teacher. He taught about two years quite a large school. His course was mostly spelling, reading, writing, arithmetic, English grammar and geography. He, however, had a class of seven in Latin. I was one of that class; and although I passed inspection in parsing lessons, yet it was all mechanical, and I do not now profess to know anything about it; and I feel confident that the same class, under the improved method of instruction, would have acquired a better knowledge of the language in three months at Lynnland Institute or Cecilia College, than our class did in two years.

Mr. Stevenson next took up tavern-keeping and then merchandising, and I think served one year in the Legislature. He was a quiet, well conducted gentleman, and a worthy man. He lived in our town perhaps ten years or more. After he left I lost sight of him.

CHAPTER XXXVII

General Duff Green was an extraordinary man, and I very much regret that my sketch of him must be very imperfect, and cannot expect to do justice to him; he was an aspiring, ambitious man, and changed his residence so often, and occupied such a conspicuous position in this world that I am not able to trace him.

He was the son of William Green, then of Cumberland county, Ky. When quite a young man, perhaps not fully of age in the year 1811, he came to Elizabethtown and made up a fine school—and perhaps followed that occupation for about two years—he was a strict disciplinarian, and in accordance with the custom of that day, made free use of the rod. He was very decisive in his measures, and used no partiality between the children of the rich and the poor—order and discipline at all hazard had to be observed. John L. Helm, the future Governor and distinguished politician was one of his pupils, and on one occasion did violate, or was supposed to violate some of the rules of the school. Mr. Green called him up, and young Helm having already developed some of the firmness which marked his future course, refused to apologize or explain—the consequence was a severe flagellation which was borne without flinching, and was the more severe on account of what Green took to be stubbornness.

Helm bore it in mind and determined in his own mind if he ever reached manhood to return the flogging with interest. It was many years after Green left before they met again. Then matters had changed; Green was high in the world, and the Governor had also attracted much public attention. When they did meet Green was the first to recognize his old pupil, and met him with such open armed cordiality that it was an affectionate embrace instead of a fight. At the time Green came to Elizabethtown I was a boy writing in the clerk's office under Major Ben Helm. Green boarded with the Major and slept with me in the office. I was then in very straightened circumstances, enjoyed the extravagant salary of forty dollars per year and board, but as I was a deputy clerk, I felt some pride in the position. But my means were so limited I was ill prepared for anything but a very scanty wardrobe. But by some means I managed to get a coat of cotton goods rather fancy colored. My father had an orchard near the office. Rather imprudently I visited the orchard with my new coat on, climbed up the tree and filled my pockets full.

and jumping out, the pockets caught in the forks, splitting my coat, and yet not to the ground—hearing the noise of the tearing, I supposed it was a rattle-snake and clapping my feet to the tree I made a desperate effort which severed my coat at the waist, leaving the apples and tail of my coat in the tree. I soon found that I was ruined, and returned to the office in a sorrowful state of mind. Green soon came in and discovered my distress, kindly offered to sell me one of his cotton coats at a nominal price.

Now, Green was nearly two feet taller than I was, but I donned the coat, which as a matter of course gave me the ludicrous appearance of a boy going to mill with his daddy's coat on. At supper time Mrs. Helm discovered the unfitness of things, and changed a coat she was making for uncle Ben and gave it to me. I considered myself a made man.

Shortly after this, date not recollected, Green volunteered in a company called the Yellow Jackets, commanded by Gov. W. P. Duvall, and went on a campaign up the Wabash against the Indians. In an Indian fight Green showed great gallantry and the horse he rode was shot in the neck. Green soon after married Miss Lucretia Edwards, sister of Gov. Ninian Edwards. She was a very handsome and admirable woman.

Shortly after he formed a partnership in the mercantile business with Major Ben Helm. Green soon received an appointment as surveyor of public lands in Missouri, and while in Missouri he was commissioned a general in the militia.

The General sold out in 1817 and went to Washington City, and soon became a favorite of General Jackson, President of the United States, and it was generally believed that he was the confidential adviser of the President and thus in an indirect manner exercised an influence in the Government. He was afterward elected to Congress and shared a good deal of Government patronage. During his residence at Washington, he visited London, and on his own hook, had an interview with a portion of the British Cabinet and suggested many items of international policy, but whether they were adopted by the Government I never learned. He is now at an advanced age if living. I have not heard of him for two years past.

was a resident of Elizabethtown about the same time that General Duff Green resided here. He kept a tavern at the same old stand where the Lion was the sign. He commenced in a log house; after some time he put up the center part of the brick building which now constitutes the Eagle House. He married one of the daughters of the late Alexander McDougal and saying that is sufficient proof that the table was first rate. He died about the year ——, and it was then considered a great loss to the town.

After his death Samuel Martin, Esq., purchased the house, and kept a hotel in good style. Martin was a natural quiz, and would try his hand upon any guest at his house even if he was the President. He is a Justice of the Peace. At the time a man was confined in jail for stealing—an acquaintance of the prisoner came to visit him and got up into the window opposite the prisoner's room, and as it afterward appeared, had implements for the prisoner to saw himself out. The jailer being absent, his wife requested the man to go away—he refused—she sent for Squire Martin—he came and took the man by the neck and pulled him down and led him to his office. He could not make out an offense for merely sitting in the window, but decided that he was a man of bad behavior in not obeying the lady, required him to give security for his good behavior, and failing to give it, he committed him to jail with the thief, but forgot to search him; so the next night the prisoner and his friend both walked out of the jail and were never retaken. Martin afterward became Sheriff by seniority under the old Constitution.

John Shackleford at one time kept the same house in good style, and afterward removed to Palmyra, in Missouri, where he kept a good hotel until his death.

Philemon Bibb also kept the Eagle House in first-rate style. Bibb and his energetic lady seemed to be natural hotel keepers. At West Point he held forth for a season and then removed to Louisville and kept the old Exchange on Sixth street for years, and no house in Louisville, for a time, surpassed it for a fine table. In those days Bibb was a very polite, obliging landlord.

also kept a hotel in this town and kept it well—was an active, energetic man. He was a moving man—lived in Hodgenville for a time and afterward removed to Louisville, where he kept at least half a dozen hotels and boarding houses, and lives there now. I cannot tell what he will go at next, for although he is growing in years and heads a large family, he will not and cannot be idle.

In my next I expect to resume a history of school teachers.

CHAPTER XXXVIII

ROBERT HEWITT,

a teacher, came to Elizabethtown in 1834. He was induced to come to this place by the late John Morris, who remained his fast friend for life. Mr. Hewitt was born in Bedford county, Virginia, on the 1st day of July, 1803, and came to Kentucky soon after his majority. His first teaching was at Hodgenville, LaRue county. As soon as he removed to Elizabethtown he took charge of the Hardin Academy and continued in charge of it until his death, February 13, 1850, and during that period of sixteen years he turned out more good scholars than any teacher before or after him. He was a ripe scholar and, according to the custom of that day, was compelled to use the rod liberally, as he had under his tuition a considerable number of hard cases, and none but a man of his determination could have governed them. He was remarkable for his modesty and unobtrusiveness—so much so that among strangers he would have passed for half his worth. But with those who knew him he was held in high esteem for his moral worth and integrity.

He was a man of clear intellect and judgment, and with intimate friends fluent in conversation and thoroughly posted on all subjects interesting to sensible men. He was of such retiring habits that he rarely sought company outside of his books, but company sought him for the purpose of enjoying the rich treat his conversation offered. He married a daughter of the late Rev. Lewis Chastain, a Methodist preacher of considerable note, who hailed from the Old Dominion, Virginia, the mother of States.

His clear judgment was so relied upon that on the occasion of a debate between the Revs. Fisher and Clark he was selected to preside as one of the moderators. He never held or sought any political office. He raised and educated several sons, and at his death left an excellent, amiable and intelligent widow, who still resides (1870) in Elizabethtown.

THE HEWITT SONS

Lafayette Hewitt, the eldest son, at the age of 18, after the death of his father, was placed by the trustees at the head of the Hardin Academy, which position he occupied with great credit for two years, when he established an independent school, which he taught until 1857. His health then became so delicate that he could not bear the confinement and went South. In 1859 he received from General Joseph Holt, postmaster general, an appointment in that department, and was assigned the superintendence of the Dead Letter Office, and resigned that position on President Lincoln's coming into power. And the war breaking out, he espoused the cause of the Confederacy and went to Richmond to engage in the war. The postmaster general of the Confederate States, learning his whereabouts, immediately telegraphed him to come on to Montgomery to aid in getting the postoffice department in working order. Accordingly he went and received the necessary appointment and went to work in earnest. When the department got into successful operation he resigned his position in order to take part in the arduous duties of the field.

On the first day of December, 1861, he received the appointment of adjutant general. A full detail of his military services is given in the "History of the First Kentucky Brigade," by Ed. Poter Thompson. That history shows that labors may be performed by a man of slender frame and feeble health when combined with a strong will and determined purpose, sustained by a brave heart.

At the end of the war he returned to Elizabethtown, May 18, 1865. He was offered the position of principal of the Elizabethtown Female Academy, of which he took charge in September, and was thus engaged for five months. He then commenced the practice of law in the courts of Hardin.

Shortly after Governor Stevenson came into office, in October, 1867, he was appointed quartermaster general of the State of Kentucky, which position he still holds.

The duties devolving upon the Captain were onerous and highly responsible, involving the settlement of four millions of dollars between the Commonwealth and the General Government, and he has acquitted himself in a manner highly satisfactory.

VIRGIL HEWITT,

familiarly called Day Hewitt, was another son of Robert Hewitt. He also was a well-educated young man, of singularly modest habits, and was withal so quiet and easy in his deportment that no one would have suspected him of wishing to engage in the toils and dangers of war. But his sympathies were decidedly with the Confederacy, and although of delicate and slender frame, he buckled on his armor and went out as quietly as if he were going into a company of ladies.

He did not go shouting and singing as some of the soldiers in the war of 1811 did. For some of them sang a song not quite up to doggerel—it hardly amounted to PUP EREL. It ran thus:

"Come all ye brave Kentuckians,
  I'd have you for to know,
That for to fight the enémee
  I'm going for to go.

And if you're freezin' for a fight,
  Come go along with me,
We'll show them for a thing or two
  In front the enemee.

If you ask where we are goin',
  I'll tell you what it means—
We're goin' on a big flatboat
  Way down to New Orleans.

And there we'll meet proud red coats,
  All heeled with golden spurs,
Though they belch big guns and bombs
  We'll thrash the Britishers."

Not so with Day. He went off decently, but he had fight in him. During the first year of the war he served with Gen. Ben Hardin Helm, and was attached to Company H in the Sixth Regiment. September 18, 1862, he was elected second lieutenant; January 12, 1863, he was promoted to first lieutenant, and October, 1863, he was made adjutant of the Sixth Regiment.

He fought at Murfreesboro, Jackson, Chickamauga, Rocky Face Ridge, Resaca and Dallas. He was wounded at Dallas, but recovered in time to take part in the battle at Intrenchment Creek, at which place he was so severely wounded as to be disabled from further service during the war. At the return of peace he came home, determined to be peaceable, and was elected county clerk of Hardin county for four years, having served in a clerk's office before the war. He made so good an officer that he has just been elected for a second term of four years.

HANNIBAL HEWITT,

the second son, was also a well educated man and partook much of the modesty of the family, and was a popular young man. He was postmaster at one time and occasionally taught school. He has been out of my sight more than the other boys, and I am not prepared to speak fully of him.

FOX HEWITT,

the fourth and youngest son, was also educated in the school of his father and his brother, Fayette Hewitt.

After Fayette went to Washington, Fox followed him. About the 1st of December, 1860, he was appointed clerk in the Treasury Department, which office he resigned in March, 1861, when President Lincoln came into office. He then went to Richmond, Virginia, and was appointed clerk in the Treasury Department of the Confederacy; this was in November, 1861.

In May, 1863, he joined the 25th Virginia battalion, and until the close of the war was in service with this battalion on the fortifications of Richmond. After the war he returned home and has acted assistant clerk of the Hardin County Court ever since that office was held by Virgil, his brother.

Thus ends a very imperfect sketch of the family of that excellent man, the late Robert Hewitt, who was one of the bright ornaments of Elizabethtown.

CHAPTER XXXIX

THOMAS JOHNSON, ESQ.,

was born in Rockbridge county, Virginia, and came to Elizabethtown about the year 1824. He commenced the practice of law, and finding it not sufficiently remunerative, got the appointment of principal of the Hardin Academy, which position he held for several years. He was an ardent man in temperament, kind and social in his intercourse, as quick as powder to resent an insult, pure in morals, but subject to low spirits. He related to me an instance of his moody habits.

One evening in winter he was walking out to relieve ennui and a heavy spirit, warmly clad, but as miserable as he could be—that is, completely in the BLUES. He met a negro on the road, barefooted and miserably clad. The negro was singing a corn song, as gay as a lark. Johnson said he was tempted to knock the negro over for pure envy, and he philosophized upon the matter. If that negro, barefooted and nearly naked, was happy, why should he, well clad and in a profitable business, indulge in such moody reflections? It cured him for that time. Johnson married a very estimable lady and removed to Texas, where he occupied a prominent position for years. Whether living or dead I cannot tell, as I lost sight of him.

REV. ROBERT L. THURMAN

was also a teacher in Elizabethtown. He was born November 19, 1815, at a point half way between Springfield and Lebanon. In the year 1819 or 1820 his father, the Rev. David Thurman, removed to Hardin county and settled at Nolynn, now LaRue county. R. L. Thurman was brought up to hard farm work—that is, while he was a boy—going to school in the winter season. He received his early education under the late Robert Hewitt, first in the country, and then followed Mr. Hewitt to Elizabethtown and was under his tuition five or six years. He then went to Georgetown College in the spring of 1839 and continued there three and a half years, and graduated in June, 1842, with the highest honors of that excellent institution.

At the age of seventeen he professed religion and united with the Baptist Church at Nolynn.

On the 25th day of July, 1843, he was ordained to the ministry, and was pastor of Severn's Valley Church, located at Elizabethtown. The Presbytery was composed of Elders Colmore Lovelace, Thomas J. Fisher, A. D. Sears and A. W. LaRue. He continued as the faithful pastor of that church for six years, and on the day after his ordination he baptized two candidates, rather a rare occurrence. During his ministry the church had a very pleasant revival. He was assisted by Dr. Gardner, then a young preacher and now located in Russellville as professor of theology at Bethel College. The last three and a half years of his pastorate he had charge of the Elizabethtown Female Seminary. For some time he had the Rev. Samuel Williams, pastor of the Presbyterian Church, as his partner, and after Mr. Thurman resigned the same school was continued by Mr. Williams for about nine months.

Mr. Thurman was married in October, 1845, to a daughter of Mr. Freeman, near Frankfort, and is now (1870) a grandfather. He removed to Louisville, and with Elders A. W. LaRue, Thomas J. Fisher and John L. Waller, the latter as senior editor, in 1852 took charge of the *Western Recorder.*

In 1851 he was appointed agent for Georgetown College and continued in that employment for four years. He then was appointed State agent for the Board of Foreign Missions and has been in that service ever since.

He is a man of untiring energy and has performed Herculean labors and done much in building up Georgetown College and in sustaining the Foreign Mission enterprises. He resided in Franklin county many years and then removed to Bardstown, where he now resides. His whole course so far has been without a blemish, and he may emphatically be termed a Christian gentleman of the first water.

Many other teachers of less note have taught in Elizabethtown.

REV. J. W. HEAGEN,

a Presbyterian preacher, was and is now a teacher.

Mr. Heagen was born in Gettysburg, Virginia. He received his education in Western Pennsylvania, and removed with his wife in 1858 to Daviess county, from thence to Breckinridge county, from thence to Bullitt county, and in 1867 he removed to Elizabethtown and took charge of the Female Seminary, which afterward became a mixed school under the title of Hambleton College.

He has proved to be an excellent and successful teacher, a strict disciplinarian, and advances his pupils rapidly. He is a man of great decision, and but very few cases of disorder have occurred in his college. He has in one or two years had as high as 120 pupils and has averaged 100 or more annually. His success has determined him to be a permanent citizen, and as an evidence of that he purchased ground and erected a large and handsome house in town, capable of accommodating many boarders.

REV. SAMUEL WILLIAMS

I have run a little ahead of my history and will drop back to the Rev. Samuel Williams, a Presbyterian preacher, who also was a teacher for a limited period. He was born in Lincoln county, Kentucky, and was principally educated at Center College, Danville, Kentucky, where he graduated.

He removed to Elizabethtown and became pastor of the Presbyterian Church in 1845, and retained that position until 1846, when he resigned.

He was the partner of Rev. R. L. Thurman, in charge of the Female Academy, and after the resignation of Mr. Thurman he continued the school alone for nine months and was considered an excellent teacher. During the most of the time of his pastorate he held services in his church every Sabbath, and finding his salary inadequate to a comfortable support, he bought a farm adjoining Elizabethtown and became rather a model farmer and had a taste for the cultivation of fruits.

During the war it was a trying time on churches and church services, yet he kept up the services regularly except for a short time, when the churches were all taken by the military and soldiers quartered in them, and the sound of a church bell was not heard for some months. It was a gloomy time for Christians. During the time of the occupation of the Methodist, Presbyterian and Baptist churches, by the special request of the wife of the writer, a prayer meeting was appointed and held in the writer's house on every Thursday night by Mr. Williams and the Rev. Dr. W. W. Lambuth, a very worthy Methodist preacher, for some months. Their punctuality in attending and their devotions at these prayer meetings were highly appreciated and have ever been held in kind remembrance by the family.

Very few men have passed through twenty-five years of active duties and trying circumstances with a more blameless life and Christian-like deportment.

CHAPTER XL

DOCTORS

As for the disciples of Æsculapius not one of them trod the soil of this town or neighborhood from the year 1780 until about 1800. It may be asked how sick folks got along in the twenty years or more. In the first place men who lived a great deal in the open air, and got their meat from the forests and glens, tender venison, the juicy bear, the substantial buffalo, the delicate turkey, pheasant, partridge, squirrel, and in place of pork, the fat possum, and these all taken in the hunt, with the rifle and hunting dogs, and all this food sweetened by toil made men healthy and they rarely got sick. In these days if a man took a cold the remedy was to drink down a half pint or pint of bear's oil—the quantity depended upon the capacity of a man's stomach, then lay down before a log fire in the woods, wrapped up in his blanket and if it snowed three or four inches deep on him in the night it was all the better, and when he awoke in the morning and shook the snow off of his blanket as the lion would the dew drops from his mane, the man was well of his cold, and fully prepared to take up his rifle and renew the hunt. If a man was taken sick in his fort or cabin the women were the doctors. Then the Elecampaign and Comfrey and Ditny tea were the sovereign remedies successfully used, and occasionally the comb of a hornet's nest was scorched before the fire and a tea was made of it, and drank without scruple, and the patient was covered up in a blanket or buffalo rug, which produced a copious sweat and worked wonders. If the hornet's nest was not to be had, sage tea was used. But a good sweat was an indispensable thing. In case of measles, which did not hurt much in those days, all the patient had to do was to keep out of the wet, unless the case was more severe than usual. Then sheep-nannie tea was prescribed; about a quart of that condiment swallowed down at night was certain to effect a cure. In case of the bloody flux, very uncommon in those days, a sovereign remedy was used, and is to this day the best of all. It was a simple remedy and always successful, and for the benefit of the present generation I will record it in my history.

RECIPE

Take about two pounds of the inner bark of the white oak tree, taken off near the root on the north side, the bark there being the thickest and strongest; put the bark in an iron vessel with a gallon of water, boil it down to a quart, then take out the bark and add a quart of new milk and a lump of sugar about the size of a duck egg, boil that down to a quart; when cooled a little it is fit for use.

DOSE

Half a common teacupful, and every two hours after two large tablespoonsful, and continued until the pains in the rectum or lower bowel cease, then hold on. But if after that the pains should return, commence again with the same treatment. But the first course generally produces the desired effect. Then let nature do her perfect work, and in a day or two the bleeding ulcers in the rectum would slough off and all pass off in the natural way, and the patient is well. Don't want to cleanse the bowels by putting calomel down the throat, for if you do unlock the liver and let down bile upon the bleeding ulcers then you might as well speak for your coffin. This course, in a practice of seventy years, always cured the disease if taken in time.

It is true some of the old ladies were a little tinctured with a superstitious notion that the bark had to be peeled upward and the water dipped upstream. But in the fullness of time that notion has been exploded. However, to do so did no harm.

One of the earliest physicians who settled in our town was Dr. Ebenezer E. Goodletter, who exercised the healing art several years in this town, and then left for parts unknown to the writer.

Then came Dr. Thomas Essex from England; he settled in Elizabethtown about the year 1809. He purchased property and was a resident for some years, and had a remarkably genteel family, and was doing a fine business until Dr. William Sulcer, a big fat Dutchman, came in the neighborhood and proclaimed himself to be the Dutch doctor, skilled in the Indian practice. He was a very illiterate man, but had a good share of common sense by nature, and he took like wildfire and swept everything in the way of practice before him, and made the natives believe that these college bred doctors were regular man killers. Dr. Essex's practice, of course, went down and he removed, if I remember right, to Tennessee.

It is an adage that "Every dog has his day," and it so happened that Sulcer had his day.

About the year 1811 Doctor Daniel B. Potter, a regular graduate, came to Elizabethtown. On his arrival he soon heard of Sulcer's fame, and he lost no time in making the acquaintance of Dr. Sulcer, and managed to get in partnership with him. They rode and practiced together. Potter flattered Sulcer and gained his good will and confidence, and Sulcer puffed Doctor Potter as a none-such and the only college-bred doctor that was worth a snap in all the land.

Those were the days of company musters and whenever a militia company was mustered in town Potter would get one or two large buckets of sweetened whisky and have the captain to parade his men before his shop, and let the whole company swig to their heart's content. This practice in addition to Sulcer's puffing and blowing about Dr. Potter soon established Potter as the King-cure-all of all the pains, aches and diseases with which the human family was prone to be afflicted. Then practice was immense, and men and women came to the conclusion that it was necessary to get sick, in order to avail themselves of his superior skill in the healing art. When firmly established he proposed a dissolution of the partnership. The consequence was that Sulcer went down like a falling star and suddenly faded away, and Dr. Potter kept the ground. Sulcer left in a short time after for a more congenial clime.

Potter soon after married Miss Hackley, a lady of surpassing beauty, and was rapidly acquiring wealth, for he was in reality well skilled in his profession, but in 1814 he fell à victim to an epidemic called the "cold plague." The writer sat up with him the night of his death, and helped to lay him out, and his death was justly considered a real loss to the community. His death left an opening which was filled by Dr. Richard A. Taylor, who enjoyed a fine practice for several years. He married a Miss Sally McGee, a very amiable lady, and after some years removed to Green county, and is now represented as a man of considerable wealth and a deserving citizen. About the time of his removal Doctors John Churchill and Christopher L. Jones, commenced the practice in partnership. Dr. Churchill was a polished gentleman, and married a Miss Percefull, who lived but a short time after her marriage. He removed to Greensburg and married a Miss Akin. Some years after his health failed and he died.

Dr. Jones removed to Harrodsburg and married a Miss Lucy May. She was a daughter of David May, a man of high respectability, and once the clerk of the Hardin Quarter Session Court.

Dr. William S. Young then commenced the practice in this town. He was a native of Nelson county, Kentucky, studied medicine with Dr. Bemiss, of Bloomfield, and was a partner of his preceptor for several years. He settled in Elizabethtown in 1814, and stood deservedly high in his profession. He was a very modest, worthy gentleman, and the late Ben Tobin, Esq., once remarked of Dr. W. S. Young, that he was the most immaculate man he ever knew. He acquired a considerable estate, was elected to Congress in 1824, and was re-elected in 1826, and died much regretted in 1827.

CHAPTER XLI

DR. BRYAN R. YOUNG

is a brother of the late Dr. W. S. Young, named in the last number. He was also born in Nelson county, Kentucky, where he was also educated. He came to Elizabethtown in 1818, and studied medicine with his brother; after graduating with honor, he was partner in practice up to the time of his brother's death, in 1827, and then continued the practice alone. He was a very successful practitioner, and had a large field to operate in, and is also a very skillful surgeon. The Doctor's skill in medicine and the healing art, and his moderate bills, made him very popular, and consequently in almost every part of the county can be found children and youths called by his name; indeed, so numerous are they, that had the Doctor thought it a duty to bestow a suit of clothes on each name-sake, it would have been a strong pull at his purse-strings. In the year 1845 the Doctor was elected to Congress, and served two sessions; and was also elected to the Legislature of Kentucky in the year 1858-59, and in 1861-62 and 1863-64, in which various positions the Doctor acquitted himself with much credit.

The Doctor is also an enthusiastic pomologist and horticulturist, and purchased a farm on Muldraugh's Hill, in Hardin county. But he has lately retired from his farm, and again has taken up his residence in Elizabethtown, and continues his practice only in special cases.

DOCTOR HARVEY SLAUGHTER

born in Nelson county, on Cedar Creek, is the son of the late Judge Slaughter, who was one of the finest specimens of an old Virginia gentleman. He resided within four miles of Bardstown, a place justly celebrated for its educational institutions, and the home of some of the most eminent lawyers in Kentucky—Judge Rowan, Hon. Ben Hardin, Hon. Charles A. Wickliffe, Hon. Benj. Chapeze, Philip Quinton, Hon. James Guthrie, and the celebrated orător, John Hays, and many others. Dr. Slaughter received his early education in Bardstown, and graduated at Transylvania University, in Lexington. He then studied medicine in the same town, under the celebrated Dr. Burr Harrison. He made his first attempt at practice at Big Spring, in 1828. But by the persuasions of our late fellow citizen, Horatio G. Wintersmith, he removed to Elizabethtown in the year 1829, and has remained here ever since and enjoyed a lucrative practice. It was the custom in this town when any man was given up by the resident doctors, to send to Bardstown for Dr. Harrison. He became tired of being sent for only to see a man die, and remarked publicly, that if Dr. Slaughter could not cure them, it was useless to send fŏr him.

The Doctor is a man of fine education and refinement, and eminent in his profession; has a fine appreciation of the poets, and is a good public speaker. He has also for a few years been engaged in horticulture, and can show as fine grapes and apples as any man in the State. In a few numbers back I have spoken of the Doctor's taste in improving his residence, rendered classic by the distinguished men who have occupied it since 1798.

THOMAS S. CRUTCHER

may be considered one of the oldest residents of Elizabethtown, now living, except myself. He was born in Bardstown, Kentucky, on the 28th day of August, 1798, just fourteen days after I was born in Elizabethtown.

His father, the late Major James Crutcher, soon after came with his family to Elizabethtown, and up to the time of his death acted a prominent part as merchant, tavern-keeper, Justice of the Peace, Judge of the Quarter Session Court, trustee of the town, trustee of the Academy, and Representative and Senator in the Kentucky Legislature. The same Thomas S. Crutcher of whom we now speak, received his early education in the same schools as myself and Thomas W. Nicholson, Rev. Ben Ogden, and Samuel Stevenson, but completed his education at Nashville, under Dr. Priestly, and boarded with Mr. Hume and roomed with John Bell and Ephraim Foster. After his collegiate course, he went as a volunteer on Gen. Hopkin's campaign on the Wabash, about Tippecanoe. He afterwards merchandised in Bowling Green, Ky., but has been for many years retired to private life, except a short period, during which he was clerk of the Hardin County Court.

HON. A. H. CHURCHILL,

another old citizen, was born near Louisville, on the 19th day of October, 1796, was educated at a school in the neighborhood, except about four months in the year 1807, in Elizabethtown, under Samuel Stevenson. In 1813 he entered Transylvania University, at Lexington, and remained there two years; settled in Elizabethtown as a law practitioner in 1818. He was elected to the Senate of Kentucky in 1832, served only one session, and receiving the appointment of Circuit Judge in 1833, which office he held with great credit to himself, and satisfactory to the community. In 1847, to the regret of his friends, he resigned that office and retired to private life.

During the time he was Judge of Hardin Circuit Court, I was clerk of the same court, and during those fourteen years I had a fair opportunity of witnessing the impartial hand with which he dealt out justice. Regardless of the state or standing of parties, he struck for law and justice. He is a man fond of the comforts of home, and the family circle, and has been married four times. He is not only a moral, but a religious man and devotes much of his time to the interest of the Episcopal Church, to which he belongs, and of which in a certain sense he is the sum and substance, as far as it concerns that body in Elizabethtown.

REV. DR. WILLIAM W. LAMBUTH

But few men have passed through more trying and difficult scenes than Dr. Lambuth. He was born near Gallatin, Tennessee, on the 9th day of February, 1832. His parents immigrated to Kentucky in 1847. Being a member of the Methodist Episcopal Church, he having been set apart to the ministry, joined the Louisville Annual Conference, at Greenville, Ky., in 1855, and traveled as an itinerant preacher until 1861. He was married to Miss Myra E. Matthis, in this town in 1858, and finding responsibilities resting upon him, he located, in 1861, and in the fall of 1862 commenced merchandising with his father-in-law, Mr. David Matthis, of this place, and continued two years, when he commenced studying medicine, which course he completed in 1866, and was graduated in both the Kentucky School of Medicine and the University of Louisville; since which time he has regularly practiced his profession, but has never given up preaching. He has also for some years been keeping a drugstore in company with Judge Cofer. The Doctor was without patrimony, and had to struggle for the means of sustenance. His time in study and the expense of attending two courses of medical lectures, were severe upon him; and yet the full trial of his faith had not come—but it did come. His aged father and mother were residing in Arkansas during the late war—the horrors of which will be long remembered. These good old people were burned out of house and home, turned out of doors, with two daughters, upon the cold charity of the world, and such was the desolation around that there were none to help but God, and they devoutly looked to Him for help, and help did come. The news of their calamity reached the ears of their son, the Doctor of whom I now write. The Doctor and his good lady thought themselves pressed hard enough already, but upon the news of their parents' disaster reaching them their hearts were enlarged, and the Doctor sped his way to the bereaved ones, and he brought the father and mother and two young sisters to his Kentucky home, and there in the bosom of his little family, they have shared together the proceeds of their joint labor to this day—except the father, who passed away in April last.

During the war the churches were all closed one winter, being occupied by soldiers, as I have heretofore remarked. It was a solemn time, no thrilling sound of the church bell was heard, to gladden the Christian's heart.

For some months Dr. Lambuth with Rev. Samuel Williams, at my wife's special request, kept up a regular prayer meeting at my house every Thursday night. However boisterous or unpleasant the night, those two men of God were certain to be on hand. These exercises were the more pleasant because of the surrounding gloom. Long will they be remembered by the family. He now speaks of joining the Conference again in the traveling connection as an itinerant preacher.

XLII

REV. WILLIAM C. JONES

Rev. William C. Jones, a Baptist minister, was born in Spencer county, Kentucky, in the year 1831. Educated at Georgetown College, where he graduated in 1858, he came to Elizabethtown in December, 1859, and connected himself with the Baptist Church and was ordained to the ministry in January, 1860, by a Presbytery composed of Dr. William Vaughan and Elders W. L. Morris and J. Toll Miller, and served the church at Elizabethtown four years, when he resigned the charge. He left Elizabethtown in 1864 and has for some time resided at LaGrange, Oldham county, Kentucky. He is now doing the work of an evangelist. Elder Jones has become an able preacher, stands high in his denomination and has scores of friends in this town.

Col. Charles D. Poston was born in Hardin county on the 20th day of April, 1825, and remained on a farm until at the age of seven years, when his father removed to Elizabethtown and conducted a newspaper, *The Western Sentinel.*

The young lad was printer's devil and news carrier in his father's office for several years, during which time he attended the school of Robert Hewitt and obtained the meagre rudiments of an English education.

In January, 1837, he entered the office of the writer and served as deputy clerk for six years. By application he soon became an expert penman and an excellent clerk. At the expiration of his term (in 1843) he went to Nashville, Tennessee, and was employed as a deputy clerk in the office of the Supreme Court. In September, 1848, Mr. Poston was married to Margaret J. Haycraft, third daughter of the writer, in whose family he had been partly raised.

For some years he was engaged in commercial enterprises with his brother, Sanford J. Poston, in Elizabethtown. These enterprises having proved unfortunate, he emigrated to California in 1850 and was employed as chief clerk in the Custom House at San Francisco for three years.

The adventurous spirit engendered by a residence on the Pacific coast, and the pressure of unliquidated debts at home, induced Mr. Poston to undertake a daring expedition into the silver mining region of Northern Mexico about the time of Gadsden's purchase, which consumed the year of 1854. The year 1855 was passed in the seclusion of his early home with his family.

In the year 1856 he started to explore the mineral regions of Arizona in the interest of the Southern Pacific Railroad, passing through the country of the Lipans, Comanches and Apaches, the most fierce and powerful Indian tribes upon the continent.

It would be difficult to find in the brilliant history of our frontier experience a more daring enterprise than this. The mining business had scarcely been inaugurated when the late war commenced. By an order from the Government the forts were burned and food of the enemy taken between California and Texas, following which the troops abandoned the country. The Mexicans and Indians caught the infection of carnage and the mining establishments were broken up amid scenes of indescribable horror. The young brother of Mr. Poston, a noble young man just arrived at manhood, was foully murdered, and nearly all the companions and employes of Mr. Poston were killed in a shocking manner. Indeed, Professor Punpelly was the only surviving companion he had left, and with him was undertaken an escape from the scenes they passed through, and the hairbreadth escapes they made in their long wilderness travel is almost incredible to relate, but by dint of cool courage and skillful maneuvering, and enduring fatigue and toil and nearly driven to starvation, they reached San Francisco in the autumn of 1861. A year or two afterward upon, the organization of civil government in the territory which he had pioneered, President Lincoln appointed Colonel Poston superintendent of Indian affairs. At the termination of this service he was elected first delegate to Congress from Arizona and served in the Thirty-eighth Congress.

In the summer of 1867, Mr. Poston made the tour of Europe. In December of the same year, at the residence of the writer, to a company of select ladies and gentlemen, his old friends and relations, he read a lecture, describing his tour and the nations he visited, in which he displayed fine descriptive powers, and at the conclusion the thanks of the company was returned through the Rev. Samuel Williams and a printed copy of the lecture was ordered. The consequence was a neat and interesting little volume was issued, entitled "Europe in the Summer Time," by C. D. Poston.

In the winter after his return he engaged for a time in the practice of law in Washington with Judge Betts, of California.

Upon the arrival of the Chinese Embassy in the United States, Colonel Poston took a lively interest in the increasing relations with that country and was appointed by the Government as special commissioner to the different countries of Asia. In this mission he was accompanied by his old friend, Ross Brown, then Minister to China.

After leaving China, where he was treated with distinguished honors by the Government, as commissioner he visited the Indian Archipelago and thence went to British India, where he was treated with distinguished consideration and furnished with every facility for traveling through that interesting country.

In the spring of 1869 Colonel Poston found himself steaming up the Red Sea under the shadow of Mount Sini and anchored over the spot where Moses led the children of Israel over the Red Sea. He remained a short time in Egypt, examining the modern wonder, the Suez Canal, and the ancient wonders, the pyramids of Egypt. He spent the summer in Europe. After having circumnavigated the globe and visited the principal capitals of Asia, he returned to New York, his temporary home, in October, 1869.

Taking a short retrospect of the life of Colonel Poston, having crossed the plains to California on two occasions and once by water, thence his escape from Arizona, after which his travels around the world and among strange nations, some of which were hardly civilized, and the number of his companions in Arizona who were murdered, we are compelled to come to the conclusion that he wore a charmed life.

MRS. WILLIAM D. VERTREES (In.)

Among those who have left an impression upon Elizabethtown and its people and one of those who stands out most distinctly was Mrs. William D. Vertress, or "Miss Eliza" as she was known to all of the children and most of the adults. Her maiden name was Eliza Ann Haynes. Her father was Dr. John Haynes, of Virginia, who was a graduate of medicine of either Harvard or Yale Medical School, and her mother was Martha Ann Campbell, of Massachusetts. They were married in Virginia and came across the mountains to Kentucky and settled at Big Spring. Eliza Haynes was born at Big Spring, October 3, 1824. In November, 1854, she married William D. Vertress, a Mexican War veteran and later county judge of Hardin county. She was the first graduate of Bethlehem Academy. Mrs. Vertress was an active, highly intelligent, educated woman, a skillful musician, and unusually well read in the best literature. She was a Christian woman who was interested in everything for the good of the town and its people. Because of her unusual mental and personal qualities she was one of the town's most beloved characters. Nearly all persons in Elizabethtown, in middle life or beyond, who know anything of music got their grounding under "Miss Eliza" and have her among their fond recollections.

Mr. and Mrs. Vertress had four children—Haynes, Martha, Charles and Catherine. Mrs. Vertress survived her husband and three of her children, and died at the home of her daughter, Catherine V. Young, at Oakmont, Pennsylvania, on January 30, 1911.

CHAPTER XLIII

It has been suggested by some, that I have failed in my history to point out the bad characters who have figured upon the stage of action in and around Elizabethtown, and have mostly confined myself to men of good character. That to a certain extent is true. There were bad men, and some of them who suffered capital punishment have been spoken of, and there might have been named also Simon Lundry, who killed his wife in a drunken fit, and was hung for it. He resided about ten miles from town and when sober was a kind husband. Also John Coyle, who passed for an Irishman, but was really a Swiss. He was a Greek scholar, but the roughest man of education I ever knew. He was suspected of killing his wife, and was hung for killing Stephens.

He professed to be a Catholic, and availed himself of the services of more than one priest. On one occasion he was visited by a citizen to whom Coyle remarked, "On this day week (being the time fixed for his execution) I will be in Abraham's bosom, and then hope to see all my enemies brought up before God and punished." His visitor said, "Mr. Coyle, if you indulge in malice in your heart, can you expect to see God in peace? You must forgive your enemies." Coyle reflected a moment and then remarked, "Well, I forgive them for they are a damn trifling pack, and not worth hating." Notwithstanding the absolution he received, he died a perfect heathen.

After the verdict was found against him, and sentence was about being pronounced the Judge asked him if he had anything further to say, why sentence of death should not be pronounced. Coyle arose, pulled off his coat and vest and rolled up his sleeves and took off his shoes. The Judge remarked, "You need not strip." Coyle said he was warm. All this time he kept his eye on a large iron poker that was leaning against the stove. I saw that it was evidently his intention to seize the poker and fight his way out. I removed the poker. Coyle then commenced a speech, in which he reflected upon the Judge and Mr. Hardin, who prosecuted, then upon all the witnesses, denouncing them as liars, that he was only guilty of manslaughter and not murder. He warned the Judge that he would visit him in his bed-chamber, and that as soon as his spirit was released from his body, he would choke Mr. Hardin to death and that each of the jurymen should receive a visit. The sheriff, standing by, requested that he might have a call, and Coyle promised to accommodate him.

So might also be mentioned Spencer, who was hung for killing his step-son, and two negroes for committing outrages upon females, and another negro for chopping off his mistress's head with an axe while she lay asleep; Wm. Hardin, who was sent to the penitentiary for killing Matthias Brandenburg; another for stealing sugar, and various other kinds of lighter crimes, and some lashed at the whipping-post. But be it remembered that none of those offenders were actually residents of Elizabethtown.

Candor also compels me to acknowledge that many of these persons of whom I have highly spoken, had some private foibles such as are common to the natural depraved nature of the human family, and against which men and women of the highest culture, the brightest intellects and purest in morals, have had to contend and to grapple as with a giant. But time, long time, has woven itself into a mantle of charity and their good deeds are only remembered. I do not feel willing to adopt the sentiment of Mark Antony in his speech over Caesar's body that, "The evil that men do, lives after them, the good is often buried with their bones," but would rather adopt the language of the poet, who sang:

> " 'Tis distance gives enchantment to the view,
> And lends the mount its azure hue."

Under the head of

DOCTORS

I discovered that I omitted to mention Doctor James Middleton, from Scotland, his native home, where he graduated, and settled in this town many years since, date not now remembered. He was a skillful physician and enjoyed a good practice. He married a Miss Briscoe, built a house and was a citizen with us for several years. The remains of the Doctor and his wife now rest in our town cemetery, but without a stone to mark the spot, and it is more than likely that no man beside myself could point out their graves.

PREACHERS AGAIN

A number of years since George Rogers, who was a wheelwright and chair maker, settled in Elizabethtown, owned property and carried on his trade. He was a worthy member of the Methodist church and became a minister in that denomination. I do not remember that he ever joined the traveling connection of that church. But after removal the Rev. Benjamin Ogden was nearly alone in the town as a cross bearer of his church and had much to contend with almost single handed. But notwithstanding the odds against which he had to contend he maintained his integrity so as to cause even his enemy to respect and like him, an instance of which I have heretofore given in speaking of the late John Morris who, in his young days, although not on speaking terms with Rogers, thrashed a man severely for cursing the preacher in the street.

Mr. Rogers came to Elizabethtown when a young man and resided here many years, then removed to Bullitt county, where he still resides, and is now an old man. If it is an offense to say so, George, I beg pardon.

JACOB ELIOT, ESQ.

also was once a citizen of Elizabethtown and played such a conspicuous part as to deserve special notice.

He was born on the second day of September, 1803, in Otsego county, New York, where he received his early education, which was but limited as his father died when he was very young. He came to Kentucky in the year 1818 and in 1828 settled in Elizabethtown and published a newspaper called the "Kentucky Statesman." He resided in Elizabethtown nine years—was part of the time jailer of Hardin county.

Some political question got him into a street difficulty with Mr. George Roberts, an attorney, on which occasion he shot Roberts in the back with a pistol for which he was tried but triumphantly acquitted. During his stay he was an active, useful citizen and became a useful member of the Baptist church. His house was a preacher's home and he was otherwise a liberal entertainer. In the year 1837 he removed to Louisville and became a partner of the late Shadrack Penn in publishing the "Louisville Advertiser," a Democratic paper that for many years measured arms with the late George D. Prentice of the "Louisville Journal."

In the year 1842 he was employed by a company largely interested in Texas lands to go to that state and attend to their interests in perfecting their title and ascertaining its value. Mr. Eliot was admirably qualified for his business, having a clear head and discriminating mind and withal a man of unflinching courage, and that last qualification was necessary on account of the dangers from Indians and other enemies incident to a new country far from the center of civilization. He went as high as the Cross Timbers in Peter's Colony, now Dallas county. Here he dug out a kind of boat and descended the Trinity river to Buffalo Bayou and perhaps was the first white man that explored that river. He afterward made out a report of the river and the country through which it ran and published it in a London paper.

He became largely interested in these lands and in the year 1849 removed to Texas and settled in Corsicana, Navarro county, no inconsiderable place, where he yet resides. He was mainly active and instru-

mental in settling that portion of the state, has undoubted influence and is now United States commissioner by appointment. His life has been an eventful one and much checkered, and this short sketch gives but a very imperfect account as his long residence in Texas, and for many years almost inaccessible, forbids the idea of giving a correct account of him, such as might perhaps fill a volume.

CHAPTER XLIV

JACOB ELIOT AGAIN

My attention has been drawn to my version of Eliot shooting George Roberts. It was stated in a careless manner and in such a way as to compromise the living and the dead. I simply said that Eliot shot Roberts in the back. On that occasion both individuals displayed true courage. Roberts attacked Eliot with a club or heavy walking stick, striking him across the bridge of his nose, knocking it quite flat. In the meantime Roberts lost his cane and ran to pick up a rock to throw at Eliot. Several persons were attempting to hold Eliot, who had drawn his pistol. Eliot, by extra exertion, threw off those who were attempting to hold him and fired at Roberts, who was some twenty-five or thirty feet off, in a stooping position picking up a rock. The ball struck Roberts on the side, ranging on the back. Then they were separated, both showing good pluck.

BLACKSMITHS

at this time all cannot be named. One-eyed Jake Blink was a gunsmith and blacksmith in the early history of the town. John Ferguson was also a blacksmith—cut no considerable figure except that he was the grandfather of Usher F. Linder, Esq., at this time in Chicago. Linder became a lawyer of considerable eminence, was an able debater and sometimes eloquent. He practiced law in Hardin for several years and then left for Charleston, Ill., in which State he served in the Legislature and was elected Attorney General of the State.

David Vance and Jack Quick were blacksmiths. John Rodman was also a fine blacksmith.

Daniel M. Williams, born within two miles of this town, served his apprenticeship in Nelson, and about the year 1812 opened a shop in this town. He was an industrious, hard working man and made things move. In winter his hammers rang until 9 o'clock at night and at 5 o'clock in the morning the well-known ring of his hammers awakened the sleepy neighbors. His wife was made of the same industrious stamp and the breakfasts were eaten by candlelight. When clerk of two courts I boarded at his house one year with my deputy, Wm. Fairley, Esq., and that year seemed to fix my early habits of rising.

The result was Williams, by honest industry, accumulated enough to buy an excellent farm on Middle Creek, where, as a prosperous farmer, he lived in high style, exercising the rights of hospitality as true Kentuckians in his day were famous for. But some few years ago he died, leaving a comfortable estate.

JAMES COOK,

an Englishman, was an excellent blacksmith, and carried on his trade extensively for several years, say from about 1815 to about 1825, when he died in the prime of life.

JAMES HAGEN

Soon after came James Hagen. He carried on his smithing several years and moved to the country, where he died.

JOSEPH SWEETS

might be said to come next. A good, smooth and an accommodating, honest man; still continues the business. He is very fond of turkey hunting and as evidences of his trophies in that way he has nailed up to a joist a row of turkey legs more than any other man in town can boast of. Joe has had so much turkey that it is a wonder he has not grown fat, but he still continues in the race horse order. He is a quiet, worthy citizen.

Many other blacksmiths of ancient date might be named, but they made no particular mark, rendering it unnecessary to mention them.

MERCHANTS

I have already named the most of them, but there is one man that deserves notice.

LEWIS HELM

was born on Hardins Creek, Washington county, and when a child his father moved to Sugar Tree Run, in Breckinridge county, about the year 1819, where Lewis spent the first few years of his life. After his brother, the Hon. John B. Helm, got established in business, Lewis entered his store and afterward became a partner and continued business with various partners till shortly before his death in 1828. He was a fine specimen of a Kentuckian, tall and of large frame, of commanding appearance; in fact, one of the finest looking men in Kentucky, and was universally popular. But notwithstanding his manly form and in early life his excellent health promising long life, he was taken off in the prime of life, leaving a handsome estate.

COL. Q. C. SHANKS,

now of Hartford, Ohio County, a son of James Shanks, once surveyor of Bullitt county, was not actually a resident of Elizabethtown but was a frequent visitor.

He raised the Twelfth Kentucky regiment of cavalry and was attached to the brigade of Gen. Harlan. He was in the flight with Gen. Morgan at the Rolling Fork in January, 1863. He had in his possession the compass and chain used in laying out the city of Louisville. They were formerly owned by Wm. Peyton, who presented them to him in memory of his father, who was his old companion and acted together in surveying in early and dangerous times.

I have now gone further in particularizing individual citizens than I originally proposed to do and my limits will necessarily compel me to leave out the names of many worthy men who in their day walked in our midst and filled up a space which without them would have been void, or I might have mentioned the names of John Park, David Weller and Joseph J. Hastings, who for many years were good citizens and active members of the Presbyterian church, who have gone to their reward.

Also Geo. Matthis, John Quiggins, Merideth Arthur and R. D. Geohegan, now living and pillars of the Methodist Episcopal church.

Also Samuel L. Hodgen, a zealous and godly man of the Christian church (better known as the Campbellite church), and his wife, Ann E. Hodgen, Mrs. Poston and Eliza Vertrees, members of the same church, all now living except the first named, S. L. Hodgen, who was called home to his reward some years since.

I would with much pleasure have given the dates of the formation of the Methodist, Presbyterian, Episcopal and Catholic churches, but have not been able to obtain the information, although I have frequently applied to the officials of these churches, and if at a future period, before I close this history, I am furnished the data I will give it publicity.

I shall, in my succeeding numbers, turn my attention to the bar, or the attorneys who, in early years, practiced law in the courts of Elizabethtown.

CHAPTER XLV

HEZEKIAH SMALLWOOD

was a worthy citizen whose name should not be forgotten—in fact, his monument stands in nearly one-half of the brick houses of Elizabethtown, for he made the brick of which at least one-half of the houses were composed, up to August 7, 1869. I have not been able to learn to a certainty the place of his birth, but the early part of his days were spent about Alexandria, Virginia, near the District of Columbia. But as the people of the United States are noted for their roving or adventurous disposition and very few men, like myself, live all their lives where they were born, but generally seek some other place to live than the place of their birth, that is not at all surprising when we remember what a vast country we have—yes, room for all, and thousands of thousands, if not millions, more, and multiplied millions upon that, and heretofore the free laws and institutions of our country permitted the inhabitants to migrate from place to place until the spot was hit upon to suit the fancy of the individual seeking a home for life. Indeed, it was not uncommon for a man to settle down, open a farm and raise a large family, and then seek some place where he could have more room for expansion. In old England, where the population is dense and the habits of an old settled country established, it is common for generation after generation to occupy the same place and follow the same pursuits, descending from father to son and from son to grandson, down, down, down for hundreds of years, but not so in our land of such extensive range.

So friend Smallwood emigrated from his birthplace and the first location I find him in, is Buffalo Creek, two miles from Elizabethtown, in the year 1802, but he must have been about for some time before, for in the ardor of his youth he had wooed and won the hand of a Miss Frankie Owens. Her parents, fearing to trust their daughter to the hands of a stranger, objected. But bolts and bars are not so constructed as to keep lovers apart. She went with him in open daylight from the paternal roof and, although a policy not always safe, she fell into the arms of one of the most affectionate husbands that ever lived. While living on Buffalo Creek he made a small kiln of brick for my father, and at the age of ten years I had the honor to break off the brick from the moulder's table, assisted by a younger brother. This was the second attempt to make brick in this town. It was looked upon as a great curiosity. One single mould was used, and twenty-five hundred brick a day, besides edging up and breaking, was considered a splendid day's work.

Rev. Ben Ogden, a Methodist preacher, had about twenty-five hundred brick made to burn in the same kiln. I was employed to bear off, and received for it fifty cents in silver, the first money I ever owned. A double-bladed knife was a thing I had long coveted, and without suffering the money to burn my pocket, I hastened to Major Crutcher's store and spent my half-dollar, got the double-bladed knife and then ran home in a rapture of bliss and soon had the privilege of hearing myself called A CALF.

Mr. Smallwood moved to Elizabethtown in 1806, opened a brick yard at the end of Main street and there moulded and burned brick for many years—in fact, until he had used all the dirt on his lot that was fit for brick. He then moved across the creek, built a better house and continued at his trade until death overtook him. Mr. Smallwood was strictly an honest man, and his heart was as deeply imbued with the milk of human kindness as ever throbbed in the breast of man. But at first he was a bad calculator and became involved in debt, and was actually committed to the county jail for nonpayment, that remnant of barbarous ages, imprisonment, yet resting on our books, but some friend bailed him out and, having learned from experience, he was more fortunate, paid his debts and lived comfortably the balance of his days.

On perusing an old record of the Baptist Church, I find that in July, 1802, he was appointed by the church to cite a disorderly member to appear and answer. Of course he must have belonged to the church for some time before, but the old record has a little touch of fire, and the date and manner of his reception in the church cannot be found. He died in the year 1838, having lived a consistent member of the church. His descendants are partly among us to this day (1870). His son, James S. Smallwood, a worthy man, met his death a few years since on the railroad. He left a genteel, deserving family. One of his daughters was lately married to the Rev. J. S. Gatton, the present popular pastor of the Baptist Church in this town. A grandson, John H. Stewart, Esq., is United States assessor for this county, a faithful and efficient officer. Some think he is so straight up that he leans a little back in his zeal to serve the Government in good faith.

Our old friend had another son, who now lives in Kansas, Henderson Smallwood, Esq., and report says his son, Hillary Smallwood, is elected secretary of state of Kansas, having previously served in the Senate of that State.

PRINTERS

Hon. Stephen Elliot was born in Otsego county, New York, in February, 1806. After receiving a common school education he served an apprenticeship in the printing business at the then country town about five miles east of where the city of Syracuse now stands. This town was then composed of one frame house. It would take a detective with a search warrant to find the place now, as it is swallowed up by the city. He came to Kentucky in 1823 and spent some time in that part of Breckinridge county called Quality Corner, so called on account of the settlement of a number of Virginia gentlemen, high-toned, wealthy and rather aristocratic, such as the Alexanders, Andersons, Washingtons, Browns, Fishers, Murrays, etc. They occupied a beautiful valley of rich land, where was kept up for years old Virginia in miniature, with all its proverbial hospitality, social visits and good cheer, and the usual round of Virginia sports and pastimes, and lucky was the man of leisure and decent apparel that got into their society on a favorable footing, for he was carried round from house to house and feasted at tables that literally groaned under the most precious viands of the land, including game, fowl, fish and generous wines, such as would make an epicure lick his lips and congratulate himself on his comfortable quarters.

Stephen roamed about a little, found out the names of really every man and woman on Sugar-tree run, spent a while at Natchez, Mississippi, then at Hardinsburg, Breckinridge county, and was employed in a printing office soon after he came to Elizabethtown in April, 1826.

Here he engaged in the first printing office ever established in Elizabethtown, publishing a paper called the *Western Intelligencer,* edited by John E. Hardin and published by Milton Gregg. He was afterward engaged with his brother, Jacob Elliot, in publishing the *Kentucky Statesman.* He opened a new office in the spring of 1834 and published a paper called the *Kentucky Register,* and in connection with various partners continued its publication for many years, after which he retired from the printing business and engaged in other pursuits. He is perhaps the oldest practical printer in the State. He has preserved several mementoes of the art, one of them a composing stick, which from its appearance is at least one hundred years old. It is made of brass and is worn almost as thin as paper. Another is an ancient printing press stowed away in an upper room over one of his store houses. It is part wood and part iron, called Stansberry's patent. This press was once owned by the Hon. Thomas Chilton, who published a paper on it in this town. It was then considered a great improvement on all printing presses then known.

NOW LOOK AT IT

Judge Elliot was for many years a justice of the Hardin County Court and also filled the office of city judge. He is yet an active business man of the first order of business qualities, and has lately shown good taste in the opened fronts and other improvements on his store houses on Main street, which has greatly improved the appearance of things in that quarter.

CHAPTER XLVI

In taking up my recollections of the bar or attorneys that practiced at the bar in Elizabethtown, as an impartial historian it will involve some labor and delicacy.

That history commenced in my infancy and some of it before I was born. Of course I have drawn to a certain extent upon tradition. It is not my intention to go into the history of the young fry of lawyers now at the bar, but of such as are now dead or have made history for themselves.

LAWYERS

The first lawyer that ever sat his foot in Severn's Valley in which Elizabethtown now stands was

JAMES DOHERTIE,

in January, 1793, of whom I have heretofore spoken. He came to my father's house, then in a wilderness, and being out of money, proposed to work his way and assisted in providing wood, etc., during the coming sugar-making season, which opened in February, and aided my mother and the children in making "home-made sugar." There was quite a camp on the old farm of tall, beautiful sugar trees standing thick on the ground. The undergrowth was chiefly pawpaw and spicewood.

Did any of my readers ever visit an old-fashioned sugar camp? Imagine for a furnace a trench three feet wide on a hillside, of sufficient depth for staving in wood, and a row of kettles set on the furnace and fastened around with spauls of stone and clay with a chimeny three feet high in the rear, then a half faced camp built around three sides covered with boards, with a large trough on each side to hold sugar water and sometimes a few still tubs.

Then the trees were tapped by cutting a notch in each tree capable of holding a gill, then a gimlet hole at the corner into which a small elder stalk was inserted—that was called the spile—a wooden trough under each spile of about the capacity of two gallons, which on good sugar days from a full grown tree was filled with sap about twice a day, then a gentle horse was hitched to a wood sled holding a barrel and a funnel in it made out of a gourd, and you have all the machinery used in sugar making.

Now, if none of you have ever broiled a piece of middling on a stick over the chimney of a sugar furnace, then had a tincup full of spicewood tea made of boiling sugar water, with a cold corn johnny cake or corn dodger and luxuriated upon it, you know nothing about the real luxury of life.

Sally Lunn, pound cake, rusk, even Hallent russ as the Irish cook would call it, roast beef, plum pudding and all such nicknacks eaten in houses on tables will not compare to it. Then the molasses and tacky-wax made at those camps threw every other delicacy in the shade. But I have digressed. I was going to talk about lawyers.

Well, in due time the 26th of February rolled around. The first court that ever sat in Hardin county took place at the house of Isaac Hynes in Severn's Valley. A quarter session court opened in due form of law, and then the announcement was made, "O-yes, O-yes, O-yes, silence is now commanded under the pain of fine and imprisonment while the justice of the Hardin Quarter Session Court is now in sitting. All who have suits to prosecute please enter or motions to make come forward and you will be heard. God save the Commonwealth."

Then James Dohertie left the camp, washed his face and hands, gathered a paper out of his knapsack and wended his way to this new court, showed his law license and was sworn in as an attorney-at-law, and the occurrence astonished all the men and women in the Valley. I never saw Dohertie, for it was two years and a half before I saw the light, and then he had departed to parts unknown.

THE HON. STEPHEN ORMSBY

was admitted to the bar on the 24th day of September, 1793. He was a sturdy Irishman from the old sod. Some years afterward he was appointed circuit judge and presided in Hardin several years. He lived in Louisville, and I think he died there.

WILLIAM M. LONG, ESQ.,

on the same day was appointed by the court as attorney for the Commonwealth. Each county then appointed their own prosecuting attorney and the governor did not commission them. Tradition says he was a profound lawyer and an able jurist. He also left before I was born.

JAMES NOURSE, ESQ.,

was admitted to the bar at the June term, 1794. He was said to be a good lawyer and a first-rate surveyor, and wrote a hand of surprising beauty. He was a business man and highly esteemed by a large circle of acquaintances, but in consequence of some aberration of mind he died by his own hand, leaving a family of the highest respectability, and was unusually regretted. Indeed, it was a shock upon the community in which he lived. Bardstown was his home.

was admitted to the bar in December, 1795, and must have been considered an able lawyer, as he was appointed with the judges after the formation of the Circuit Court system.

HON. JOHN POPE

was admitted to the bar on the 2nd day of February, 1796. He was born in Prince William county, Virginia, in 1770. Having when quite young lost his right arm by accident, he determined to study law and attained the very highest eminence at the bar. He removed to Kentucky and served a number of years in the Lgislature. He was a senator in Congress from Kentucky from 1807 to 1812, and after acting a part of the time as president pro tem. of that body, in 1829 he was appointed governor of Arkansas. He served as a representative in Congress from 1836 to 1843. He resided many years in the city of Lexington, but in the latter part of his life removed to Springfield, in Washington county. He was a handsome man of large stature and pleasing address, and stood as high as any man of his day as an eloquent pleader. He died July 12, 1845.

HON. FELIX GRUNDY

first came to Elizabethtown at September term, 1797. He was born in Virginia, September 11, 1770, removed with his father to Kentucky, and was educated at Bardstown Academy. He studied law and soon became distinguished at the bar. He commenced his public career at the age of twenty-two as a member of the Legislature of the State of Kentucky. In 1806 he was appointed a judge of the Supreme Court of Kentucky and soon after chief justice. In the year 1807 he removed to Nashville, Tennessee, and became eminent as a lawyer. From 1811 to 1814 he was a representative in Congress from Tennessee, and during several years he was a representative in the Legislature of that State. From 1829 to 1838 he was United States senator, and in later years was appointed by President Van Buren attorney general of the United States. In 1840 he resigned that position and was again elected senator in Congress. He died in Nashville on December 12, 1840. If all the public acts of this extraordinary man could be collected it would make a volume.

CHAPTER XLVII

In my last number I commenced giving my recollections of the bar at Elizabethtown.

And having in that number arrived at a point where I needed the knowledge of some facts I found I had omitted some professional men. For instance:

DR. JAMES W. SMITH

came to Elizabethtown about the year 1830 and remained here the balance of his life. As a physician he was a very popular man, had an extensive practice and accumulated a handsome estate. He built the Shower's house and resided in it until his death, which occurred in the year 186—. The Doctor had many warm friends, who deeply regretted his death.

HEZEKIAH SMALLWOOD AGAIN

It has been suggested to me that I should not have spoken of his imprisonment for debt. But I contend that it was proper to name it, for that made a turning point in the management of his temporal concerns. He was not imprisoned for crime or disorderly conduct, for he was well known by all as a strictly honest man and an orderly walking Christian man. But it was for debt, and how did he become indebted? It grew out of the goodness and kindness of his heart in employing more hands than was necessary to carry on his business in order that their labor might be lighter, and his generosity in giving those hands too high wages and then, through mistaken policy, feasted them too high. All these things closed in on him stealthily but steadily and caught him unawares in debt, and some Shylock must needs have his pound of flesh, availed himself of a law then in existence, a relic of barbarism and a disgrace to our statute books, and cast him into prison. Some generous friend assisted him, and having discovered the leak which sunk his ship he adopted a new policy, paid all his debts and lived in comfort the balance of his days. To say that he lived comfortably does not express the true status of his family, for if there ever was a family in which true kindness and love toward each other existed in an eminent degree it was to be found under the happy roof of Hezekiah Smallwood.

There all the generous feelings and affections existing in the family circle, embracing the connubial, parental, paternal relations were cultivated, not as a cold science, but were the spontaneous outgushings of the deeply seated and over-flowing fountains of generous souls and loving hearts.

In the number heretofore published in speaking of the descendants of the old patriarch I made an allusion to his grandson, John H. Stewart, Esq., the typesetter omitted the word ALMOST, which left some little doubt about the proper construction of the passage. I meant to convey the idea that he was a faithful and honest officer, striving to secure to the Government all that was right under the law and no more, and my remark that he was so straight up as (almost) to lean back was merely intended to give my idea of an honest officer.

One of Hezekiah Smallwood's daughters married a gentleman named William Deckar. One of his sons, Henry Deckar, lives in Owensboro, Ky., a respectable young man, a strong advocate of temperance, and belongs to the Good Templars. But the paper of that city has rather pitched into him, charging him with having taken two horns and that it was a matter of record. This was rather calculated to shake the confidence of his friends in his sobriety until it was explained. He had been twice married and each time to a lady named Horn.

I have been particular in giving the descendants of my old friend, having previously spoken of Hillary Smallwood, a grandson, who was a Senator in Kansas and now elected Secretary of State, in order to show the progressive nature of our institutions and how from small beginnings and humble pretentions, where honesty and correct morals are taught and better feelings of the heart cultivated, there is, comparatively speaking, no bounds set to the attainments and prosperity of the descendants down the stream of time, flowing from such a fountain.

NEWSPAPERS AGAIN

In 1857 J. T. Phillips bought out the Elizabethtown *Intelligencer,* a "know nothing" paper which was previously published by C. G. Smith and George Parker with decided ability. When Smith and Parker sold out they went to Glasgow, where they published a paper for some time. Geo. W. Parker, Esq., on quitting that paper, removed to Charleston, Ill., where he is now a successful practitioner of law and vice-president of a railroad company.

Phillips then commenced the publication of the Elizabethtown *Democrat,* the first Democratic paper ever published in the county except a paper previously published by Chas. Hutchings many years before. In 1860 Phillips sold out his paper to Colonel, now Judge M. H. Cofer, who continued the paper until shortly before he went to the Southern Confederacy in the late war.

T. J. Phillips is now jailor of Hardin county, serving his second term, to which office he was elected by the people. In addition to which he is now foreman in the printing office of Matthis & Bell.

R. B. B. WOOD, ESQ.

In 1862 he edited a small paper called the *Democrat.* In 1865 he was junior editor of the Elizabethtown *Banner* at its commencement, and became editor of that paper on the retirement of Captain Frank D. Moffit. Some of his articles were extensively copied, especially one on General Burbridge, which was copied all over the country. He was, for a short time, local editor of the *Kentucky Telegraph* and became one of its editors. This paper was started by Mr. Barbour and for a short time was published daily.

He retired from that paper for the purpose of accepting the position of city attorney for Elizabethtown and to resume the practice of law. He has been an occasional correspondent for many papers, among which were the Louisville *Journal,* Louisville *Courier* and Louisville *Democrat,* the Nashville *Gazette* and the New York *Daily News.*

He has written some very passable poetry and continues to write occasionally for the press. He has never served a regular apprenticeship in a printing office or been printer's devil, but has been about and connected with printing offices so long that he is a tolerably fair printer. At the last election he was elected justice of the peace in the town district, and has lately been appointed by Judge Cofer as examiner for Hardin County.

CHAPTER XLVIII

In the early part of my history I commenced rather extensively on the life and character of Hon. Henry P. Brodnax.

In my fifty-third number I was taking up my recollections of the bar, remarking on each in the order in which they came to the bar. When I came to Henry P. Brodnax I made a short notice in these words:

HENRY P. BRODNAX

was a Virginian by birth, was admitted to the bar in Elizabethtown in April, 1796. On being appointed circuit judge he removed from Bardstown to Russellville, in Logan county.

As I have heretofore spoken of him I do not deem it necessary to repeat what I have already said of him.

He was a man of remarkable neatness, high toned and somewhat inclined to be aristocratic.

Then followed the words: "David Donan was also admitted to the bar in April, 1796." I never knew him, nor do I know of any man who did know him, and can only say that he was a lawyer at the bar 74 years ago.

Our clever typo, Mr. Yeager, was setting up the number, and after the words, "Brodnax was admitted to the bar in April, 1796," he cast his eyes to the street, perhaps to see a dog fight, and on turning his face to the case caught the same April, 1796, under the name of Donan, and followed him out, which made me cut the acquaintance of my old friend the Judge, under whose eyes I had drawn hundreds of pages of record.

This omission attracted the attention of my old friend, Mark Hardin, of Shelbyville, Ky. He is a fast man, and popped into this world 14 years before I did, is as sound as a rock, writes without spectacles, and has a memory like a book, and he began to take notice of things 14 years before I did and for my tardiness in coming to taw he has once or twice given me a raking down. But seeing that the printer had made me say that I never knew Brodnax and that I had never seen anybody that did know him, he came to my rescue in the following letter:

Shelbyville, 7th February, 1871.

Sam'l Haycraft, Esq.

My Dear Old Friend: Will you permit me to come to the rescue? "You know nothing of Henry P. Brodnax, and I never saw anybody that did." I pretend not to remember the date, but the first time I saw him, in the summer, he had on a coat made of white ribbed dimity. The skirts nearly touched the ground, the pockets were on the outside—white cassimere short breeches, knee buckles, silver with weighty sets, in pure glass, or like glass, very fine cotton stockings, hair powdered and tied behind, very light hair, light eyes and thin white skin, finely formed, and fully common sized man, always dressed neat, had some peculiarities if not eccentricities, rather holding himself above the commonality. He was made one of our circuit judges and settled in Russellville and for a time in Logan county in the country.

He became an active, zealous Cumberland Presbyterian, built a church at his own expense, on his own land, and was very active in the service of the church.

He had enemies and the house of worship was burned down. Eventually he joined the Old School Presbyterian church. He never married and by his will, as he had received nothing from his family, so he chose to will a large portion of his property to be devoted to the education of the needy, upward of twenty thousand ($20,000) dollars was appropriated to the Brodnax professorship in the Theological Seminary at Danville some time between the years of 1850 and 1860.

There is a monument to his memory erected in the cemetery at Russellville, 1859. So much to replace or to refresh the vacuum which time has blotted from your memory. I thank you for yours of December.

Your friend,

MARK HARDIN.

I am inclined to thank the printer for skipping 13 lines, as it was the means of supplying me with items before I knew the Judge. My knowledge of him did not run back to the dimity coat and I lost sight of him before he left the Cumberland and joined the Old School Presbyterian and made them that liberal donation. I thank my old friend Hardin as it began and finished out the portrait of Judge Brodnax in handsome style.

GABRIEL JOHNSON, ESQ.

was admitted to the bar in October, 1797. He lived in Louisville and ranked high among the profession, and I regret that I have not the means of taking a more extensive notice of him.

It is an old saying that a man can be judged by the company he keeps. In October, 1797, when Johnson was admitted to the same term with Governor Edwards, there was a suit pending in the Hardin Quarter Session Court, of Joseph Barnett's against Robert Baird's heirs, involving the title to lands in what is now Ohio and Daviess counties, and now worth a million dollars. Even then, at the low price of land, it was deemed of great importance and it was thought by the representatives of the parties that the greatest legal talent should be employed in an arbitration of the matters in suit, and accordingly Henry P. Brodnax, John Rowan, Felix Grundy, John Pope, Ninian Edwards and Gabriel Johnson were chosen as the arbitrators. They constitute the ablest body of referees ever appointed in Kentucky to decide a law suit. Indeed, they would have constituted a strong commission in settling the question between Prussia and France, and either of them would have made a fair president of the United States, as their after history has fully proven.

Richard Harris, Esq., was sworn in at the bar in April, 1798.

SAMUEL BRENTS, ESQ.

was a resident of Green county, Kentucky, was admitted to the bar April, 1800. He was a lawyer of considerable note, was frequently elected to represent his county in the Legislature of Kentucky, had an extensive and lucrative practice. He died of cholera at his home in Greensburg in the year 1832 or 1833.

CHAPTER XLIX

ALEXANDER POPE

was admitted to the bar in April, 1803.

He was a son of William Pope and a younger brother of Gov. John Pope. He was a well educated gentleman and a good lawyer and for many years was the prosecuting attorney for Hardin county.

He was highly social and companionable and of peculiar modesty —such as was not common to his profession, and of great amiability. But in early life he was seized with an incurable disease. With the hope of relief he visited Eastern cities and was informed by the ablest physicians that his was a hopeless case.

One of our most intelligent merchants accompanied him home from Philadelphia and found Mr. Pope, notwithstanding he looked upon his days as numbered, to be a social and agreeable traveling companion. On arriving at home at Louisville he patiently and pleasantly awaited his time without a murmur and passed away in the meridian of his manhood, at his residence, with his family and friends around him.

JOHN W. HOLT

was admitted to the bar in March, 1802. Mr. Holt settled in Elizabethtown and was one of our citizens for a few years. He was a quiet, unobtrusive gentleman and found that the practice of law did not suit his pacific disposition, retired from the practice and settled on the Ohio River, in Breckinridge, near Stephensport, and was for years a successful farmer. He lived and died in great tranquillity and was the father of Dr. Richard Holt and Thomas Holt, the latter now occupying the old homestead. He was also the father of Judge Advocate General Joseph Holt, of Washington city.

DAVID TRIMBLE

was admitted to the bar at the July term, 1803. I am not prepared to give any definite account of him.

WORDEN POPE, ESQ.

was sworn in as a practicing attorney at the bar of this county in October, 1803. He was born on Pope's Creek, Virginia, in the year 1772. His father was Benjamin Pope, brother of Wm. Pope, who also came to Kentucky with his family, and from the two brothers, Benjamin and William, sprang all the Pope family in Kentucky.

Worden Pope came to Kentucky with his father in the year 1779, and first settled in Louisville, but owing to its unhealthful condition and its water at that time, his father, believing that the land on Salt River was as good as Bear Grass land, and not having the remotest idea of the future city and its improved condition as to water and health, purchased land on Salt River and settled about a mile and a half below Shepherdsville, in Bullitt county. The farm is now owned and occupied by his grandson, Jas. Y. Pope.

Benjamin Pope established a ferry across Salt River at Shepherdsville and put his son, Worden Pope, of whom I now write, in charge of the ferry. While thus employed it chanced that the Hon. Stephen

Ormsby, who was then clerk of the Jefferson Circuit and County Courts, passed that way and was rowed across Salt River by young Worden Pope. Ormsby, who was afterward Circuit Judge and a member of Congress, was attracted by something about the young ferryman and drew him into conversation, and seeing at once that he had a mind far superior to common ferry boys told him that if he would come to Louisville he would make a man of him, and on reporting the conversation to his father consent was obtained for Worden to go to Louisville, and he determined at once to accept Mr. Ormsby's offer. But going to Louisville to live required a little outfit, or rigging out, and this was soon accomplished, and so arraying himself in a coonskin cap and a pair of buckskin moccasins and a pair of corduroy pants—I never ascertained to a certainty what supplied the place of coat, but it is most likely and almost certain that it was a dressed buckskin hunting shirt. And my preference is that it should have been so. Thus equipped, he footed it through the woods to Louisville. As the city was then a small town he soon found the clerk's office and commenced writing under Judge Ormsby, and from that day until the day of his death he was never idle, boy or man. I knew him for about 30 years and can testify that I never knew a man of more patient industry and constant application to business. In the year 1796 Judge Ormsby resigned the clerkship in both courts and Worden Pope was appointed and held both offices until 1834, when he resigned the Circuit Court clerkship and held on the County Court until his death, April 20, 1838. He was a regular practitioner at the bar in Elizabethtown and boarded with Major Ben Helm, the clerk, with whom I lived. His habit at Court time was to come to the office very night and, if not professionally engaged, would sit by me for hours and dictate the forms as I drew up the orders of court, and it was mainly to him that I was indebted for what clerical knowledge I possessed. He took considerable interest in me, for which I have always been thankful. He was a fine historian and when I received the appointment of clerk he urged upon me the necessity of reading, and particularly historical works, and furnished me a list which I purchased and have in my library to this day.

The proceedings of the Louisville bar after his death are so just and true that I will, without comment, give those proceedings, to-wit:

"At a meeting of the judge and members of the Louisville bar, and the officers of the courts, on the 21st day of April, 1838,

"On motion of the Hon. J. J. Marshall, the Hon. George M. Bibb was called to the chair, and on motion of Henry Pirtle, Garnet Duncan was appointed secretary, and the following preamble and resolutions were offered by the Hon. John Rowan (after announcing his death the preamble reads):

"He came to Kentucky in the year 1779 and, after encountering the hardships and sharing the dangers incident to the condition of the country he availed himself of the limited means of education then accessible to inform his mind and qualify himself for future usefulness. Endowed by nature with a good constitution and a vigorous mind he improved the former by manly exercise and enriched the latter by zealous and unremitting devotion to the attainment of solid and useful information. Without the aid of a classical education he acquired a thorough and accurate knowledge of literature. He was not a man of showy or ornamental display. In the profession his strength was in the extent and accuracy of his knowledge and the soundness of his judgment. He was temperate in all his enjoyments, patient of labor and research in whatever he was engaged, benevolent and charitable in a high degree, or moral firmness and sincerity and friendship, his enmities were slow in forming and swift in fading; his manners were neither gracious nor repulsive; he had an habitual aversion to artificial or fictitious mannerism; his manners and morals were formed in the old school where the solid was preferred to the showy and where stimulated courtesies were rebutted by honesty and sincerity of sentiment. Influenced through life by sentiments of that school and the inherent benevolence of his own heart and feelings, his powers and attachments were devoted more to the benefit of society than of himself. As clerk he was in a position to be consulted by the widow, the orphan and the indigent, and his knowledge of law enabled him to obey the kind impulses of his nature and beneficially to the applicants.

"Although he possessed the facilities for speculation beyond everybody else, he never touched it, so that it may be said of him emphatically he lived for others, not for himself.

"These facts of his life constitute his best eulogy and the more there shall be known of him the more his loss will be deplored and his memory revered."

Worden Pope deserved every word of praise contained in the resolutions.

He was a profound lawyer and perhaps one of the best lawyers in the State. He was engaged in the United States Court in Kentucky in one of the most important cases ever tried in the State. The whole of the city of Louisville and adjacent lands was involved, worth millions. In that case Judge Mills and Robert Wickliffe were the opposing counsel. He succeeded in the case. It was appealed from, but in consequence of Mr. Pope being very nearsighted by day and totally unable to see at night he was prevented from arguing the case at Washington.

He was personally devoted to, and intimate with the President, General Jackson. On the first election of General Jackson he offered Mr. Pope any appointment in his gift, but with his usual disinterestedness he declined by saying that he would be satisfied if Governor John Pope was promoted to the Supreme bench. He practiced law in the counties of Bullitt, Oldham, Hardin, Nelson and Meade.

In consequence of a fall he was paralyzed, which occasioned his death.

The length of this number prevents my saying anything about his descendants.

CHAPTER L

APOLOGETIC

Business of importance of public and private character over which I had no control has caused me to suspend my history from the 23rd day of March past. I hope in future to be more regular until I close.

GOV. WILLIAM P. DUVALL

was admitted to the bar in Elizabethtown in October, 1804.

He was born in Virginia in the year 1784 and there received his education. In his youth he was a little inclined to be wild; he was fond of a gun, a chicken fight and a horse race. While but a youth he determined to come to Kentucky and so announced to his father. A consultation was held as to what should be his outfit. His father remarked,

"If I give you a negro you will sell him the first chance and spend the money you get for him; if I give you a horse you will bet him off at the first horse race you see, and if I give you a pocket full of money you will bet it off or give it away. You love a gun and would not part with that."

So it finally wound up by giving him a strong suit of clothes fitted for the woods, a gun with ammunition, a knapsack with a shirt or two, and other light fixings.

With a light heart he took leave of his many relatives and told them he would never come back until he was a member of Congress. So he footed it over the mountains and through forests, crossing many rivers, and his only companion was his trusty rifle, which for a great portion of the travels furnished his food.

He arrived at Bardstown, Kentucky, and there halted, being satisfied that was a good place for him, laid aside his gun and commenced the study of law under Judge Brodnax, and during the time of study fell in love with and married a daughter of Col. Andrew Hynes. Colonel Hynes was the founder of Elizabethtown, and the town was name in honor of his wife, Elizabeth Hynes.

Duvall, having sown his wild oats, devoted himself to his studies and soon commenced the practice of his profession. As no lawyer then resided in Elizabethtown, he was appointed county attorney of Hardin county and was a regular practitioner in the courts of the county until 1822.

In the year 1812 he became candidate for Congress, and such was his general popularity that no one opposed him. He served in Congress in 1813-14. On his first trip to Washington he visited his relatives in Virginia for the first time after leaving there, thus verifying his promise that he never would return to Virginia until he came as a congressman.

In 1822 he was appointed governor of Florida by President Monroe, and was reappointed by Presidents Adams and Jackson. While attending court in Elizabethtown in 1810, 1811 and 1812 he boarded at the house of Major Ben Helm, as also did Worden Pope and Fred W. S. Grayson. I was then a lad, acting under Major Ben Helm as deputy clerk, and sat at the same table, and it was a feast to listen to their pleasant conversation and sallies of wit.

Governor Duvall was the very life of the social company, always humorous and pleasant, and was a good parlor singer. He was, in fact, one of the most generous hearted, liberal men that I ever knew, and his house in Bardstown was the seat of hospitality. But in his advanced years he was not without his troubles. His two sons, Burr H. Duvall and John Duvall, were soldiers in the war between Texas and Mexico and belonged to the command of Colonel Fannin. That whole command were taken prisoners by the Mexicans. After detaining them two days they were marched out with a Mexican regiment by the side of them under the pretense they were to be removed to some other post. Two young Mexican officers who had been educated at St. Joseph College at Bardstown, and well acquainted with the young Duvalls and often enjoyed the hospitality of Governor Duvall, promised ample protection to the young men, but proved faithless. After they had marched out clear of the encampment they were halted in line and the Mexicans ordered to fire upon them. At the first fire nearly all of Fannin's men fell dead. Burr H. Duvall and Jefferson Merrifield, also a Kentuckian, fell dead. About four hundred men were thus brutally massacred. As if by a miracle John Duvall was not hit, and he ran for life with a squad of Mexicans after him until they reached a river. John plunged in and swam across amidst a shower of musket balls, but escaped unwounded. He traveled several days without food and finally reached home.

In the year 1848 the Governor moved to Texas and died at Washington City, March 19, 1854.

At the same term William Watkins and George Strauther were admitted to the bar. They continued but a short time, and I can give no satisfactory account of them.

Judge Henry Ravidge was admitted to the bar at April term, 1805. He did not continue long at the bar, but was promoted to the judicial bench in one of the lower circuits of the State. He was an amiable man of excellent character.

HON. BEN HARDIN

was admitted at the July term, 1805, being the twenty-first lawyer sworn in the court at Elizabethtown. He was born in West Morland county, Pennsylvania, in the year 1784.

He was a son of Ben Hardin, who married Sarah Hardin, the eldest sister of Col. John Hardin, of whom I have heretofore spoken at length.

The Hon. Ben Hardin, of whom I now write, might be said to be all Hardin, as his father and mother were both Hardins and first cousins.

Mr. Hardin when a boy received his first lessons in education under Ichabod Radley, and then at Bardstown under Daniel Barry, an Irish linguist.

Barry was an irritable man and in a controversy with Gilpin, a silversmith, Gilpin killed him. After Barry was tried he removed to Hartford, now in Ohio county, and Mr. Hardin followed him to that place as the best chance then in Kentucky to obtain an education, at least a knowledge of the dead languages. Having completed his education, he commenced the study of law under Gen. Martin D. Hardin on the first day of April, 1804, at Richmond, in Madison county, Kentucky. At the April term of that court he became acquainted with William T. Barry, Samuel Woodson, George M. Bibb, John Pope and William Owsley.

According to Mr. Hardin's account of himself, he was humble and obscure. He had been an ambitious student and was of slender build, with very little flesh, so much so that his comrades called him "Tushy Works," but in after life when fortune smiled upon him he became stouter and exhibited quite an imposing appearance, his critics then respecting him, for which he was much gratified, and the friendships thus formed lasted until his death with Berry, Pope, Woodson and Bibb. Not so with Owsley. On April 1, 1805, he returned to Bardstown and studied law under Felix Grundy. In June, 1806, he obtained his law license.

The fact that he commenced his law studies in April, 1804, acquired a thorough knowledge of ancient history, and laid the foundation for one of the most profound lawyers in Kentucky or elsewhere, got married to a Miss Barbour and removed to Elizabethtown and was sworn in as an attorney in July, 1806, is proof sufficient that he was a hard student.

Mr. Hardin resided in Elizabethtown not quite two years. A man named William Bray, living in the upper end of Hardin county, killed a man and was charged with murder. Some friends of the accused came to town and employed Mr. Hardin to defend Bray, and were free to inform him that they wished him to take charge of the case until the big lawyers came down from Bardstown. Those few words decided the case with Mr. Hardin. He went to his place of residence and told his wife to pack up with all speed and moved to Bardstown, for he never would be called a great lawyer until he did so, and before Bray was indicted at the spring term, 1808, Mr. Hardin was a resident of Bardstown, Kentucky, and remained so until his death.

www.ingramcontent.com/pod-product-compliance
Lightning Source LLC
LaVergne TN
LVHW050641100826
845148LV00011B/1937

9781596412002